BUILDING A CULTURE OF CONSCIOUS LEADERSHIP

A significant driver of disengagement amongst employees is a lack of psychological safety generated from weak and underdeveloped intra- and interpersonal skills on the part of managers. Addressing the issue head-on, this book enables leaders to lead with conscious awareness to build and sustain psychologically safe cultures through which team members may positively engage with work in a far more meaningful and purposeful way.

All too often, leadership-follower relationships are purely transactional and focus on errors and problems, resulting in an impoverished transactional leadership culture. These dynamics result in weak rapport, low levels of emotional intelligence on the part of line managers and, subsequently, employee disengagement. This book unpacks these drivers in detail and builds a model that can be used as the basis of personal development and as a large-scale intervention into the leadership culture of an organisation. This model is very accessible and can be used in a structured training programme through a series of action learning workshops based upon coaching relationships and mutual dialogue.

The book is ideal reading for HRM managers, change leaders, learning and development managers, students of management and leadership, and line managers in organisations who are involved in leadership roles.

David Potter is the founder of The Cultural Change Company (www. culturalchange.co.uk) and holds both a PhD and an MBA specialising in organisational cultural change. David has over 25 years of practice as a senior manager leading change across complex organisations.

Jens Starke is a highly skilled coach, NLP master trainer and consultant with almost 20 years of project management experience across more than 15 countries. Jens specialises in facilitating transformations within organisations to leverage project management and cultural changes for competitive advantages.

"This book is a must-read for any leader who is keen to develop and lead consciously. In this time when the world is moving away from capitalism to conscious capitalism, the demand for authentic leadership, emotional intelligence and social responsibility from the leaders has never been greater. The authors successfully argue that conscious leadership is the answer to all of the above. The book provides solid insight into the existing theory (with excellent literature review for those of us who value evidence-based research!) and a variety of practical tools that can be applied instantly in order to develop conscious leadership competencies.

Reading this book has helped me reflect on my own leadership style and the kind of leader I would like to become. I feel much better placed to take my leadership development to the next level with an aim to benefit my career, my organisation's aspirations and the experience of my team".

Gintare Geleziunaite, *Head of Change Strategy, Department of International Trade*

"There are many books on the elusive topics of leadership and positive mindset but this new publication by David Potter and Jens Starke takes a different perspective from most with its focus on the concept of 'conscious leadership'. The premise of the book is that good leadership involves building and sustaining 'psychologically safe cultures'. In approaching this, the authors set out how to lead by becoming consciously aware. By doing so, leaders can build an engaged employee culture, avoiding the traditional, transactional form of management that the authors argue is still all too prevalent.

Based on empirical research and including a review of relevant theory, this book is a comprehensive resource. It sets out guidance on how to develop a conscious leadership approach in the workplace. In that sense, the book fulfils its objective of being accessible and practical. The focus on developing reflective learning capability as a leadership tool will resonate with those managers and leaders who see the value of creating a psychologically safe culture and the benefits to an organisation and its people that can follow. Self-awareness and developing a growth mindset are the starting points to becoming a conscious and effective leader and this book is a very helpful resource for students of management, leaders and aspiring leaders".

David Levinson, *MBA Careers Manager, Adam Smith Business School, University of Glasgow*

"Reading this book gave me explicit insights to deeper grounds that are involved in the transformation of leaders into 'Conscious Leaders'.

Potter and Starke, in clear language, uncover troubling underlying streams that are present in leaders as a consequence of their lifelong training (upbringing) and subsequent beliefs. And then, more importantly, showing ways and means to transform these streams into a helpful flow. They put together sources from different fields-of-thinking that have – although sprouting from different roots – similarities and remarkable impacts, resulting in an integrative workable approach. An approach in which they come up with a method to help transform anti-conscious leaders into Conscious Leaders. Leaders who consciously take responsibility for the situation they find themselves in. Leaders who have a profound understanding of how they can tune their communication, motivation and inspiration skills to the people around them, thus creating a safe environment for all – themselves included – to live and learn.

To me personally, reading this book proved to be hugely inspiring. It provided me with a skillfully gathered heap of insights and tools that is of critical use in my own work with people who are leaders working with vulnerable target groups: (school)children and refugees; parents, teachers, psychologists and social workers.

This book put together a lot of interesting easy-to-use wisdom and tools from many coaching and spiritual high standard sources, cemented with the apparent knowledge and understanding of both writers. It's a book worth reading and working from. A gem in the collection of leadership and coaching books. Thank you David Potter and Jens Starke".

Angélique de Graaff, *NLP Master Trainer/Speaker*

"*Building a Culture of Conscious Leadership* provides an excellent source for leaders at all levels who aim to build high-performing, collaborative new generations teams. Reading this book is about learning what we do not know and what we need to know in order to be more effective leaders in our organisations. It presents a set of ideas and methods that can be understood and put into practice with little effort by anyone who is expected to fulfil a leadership function.

This book is an excellent source of theoretical and practical guidance in the field of conscious leadership that draws on ideas and practices from behavioural science, political science, psychology, and sociology.

Overall, it is an excellent book with practical exercises and learning that enables managers to reflect on their own leadership competencies and leadership culture".

Eszter Vuity, *Marketing Executive MBA, MCIM*

"The book introduces an intellectually stimulating discussion of conscious leadership through theory and practice. It explains the role of critical reflexivity in enhancing the role of leaders, as well as their awareness of their competencies. It incorporates insights from work on emotional and cognitive intelligence, and how they are inextricably connected to conscious leadership, but also how they influence other forms of leadership, transactional and transformational leadership. The book further sheds light on the notion of identity work, and how leaders can engage with different activities that inform their professional selves.

Discussions around 'meaning makers' are profoundly insightful, with conscious leaders provoking followers to socially construct and internalise shared beliefs. Although this approach is important for motivation and driving success, it is even more crucial particularly during turbulent periods that involve risks and significant change.

I see this book as an important contribution to our understanding of leadership, particularly conscious leadership. I would like to thank the authors for the effort they put into this state of the art".

Dr Rami Al-Sharif PhD/MBA (Distinction); B.Com (Hons); PGCAP;
RET-Fellow; AFHEA, *Lecturer in Human Resource Management,*
Associate Fellow of the Higher Education Academy

BUILDING A CULTURE OF CONSCIOUS LEADERSHIP

David Potter and Jens Starke

Routledge
Taylor & Francis Group

LONDON AND NEW YORK

Cover image: atakan/getty

First published 2023
by Routledge
4 Park Square, Milton Park, Abingdon, Oxon OX14 4RN

and by Routledge
605 Third Avenue, New York, NY 10158

Routledge is an imprint of the Taylor & Francis Group, an informa business

© 2023 David Potter and Jens Starke

British Library Cataloguing-in-Publication Data
A catalogue record for this book is available from the British Library

Library of Congress Cataloging-in-Publication Data
Names: Potter, David (Founder of The Cultural Change Company),
    author. | Starke, Jens, author.
Title: Building a culture of conscious leadership / David Potter and
    Jens Starke.
Description: Abingdon, Oxon ; New York, NY : Routledge, 2023. |
    Includes bibliographical references and index.
Identifiers: LCCN 2022009444 (print) | LCCN 2022009445 (ebook) |
    ISBN 9781032224916 (hbk) | ISBN 9781032224879 (pbk) |
    ISBN 9781003272793 (ebk)
Subjects: LCSH: Leadership. | Management. | Interpersonal relations.
Classification: LCC HD57.7 .P685 2023 (print) | LCC HD57.7
    (ebook) | DDC 658.4/092—dc23/eng/20220407
LC record available at https://lccn.loc.gov/2022009444
LC ebook record available at https://lccn.loc.gov/2022009445

ISBN: 978-1-032-22491-6 (hbk)
ISBN: 978-1-032-22487-9 (pbk)
ISBN: 978-1-003-27279-3 (ebk)

DOI: 10.4324/9781003272793

Typeset in Classic Garamond
by Apex CoVantage, LLC

Dedication by David Potter

I would like to thank my mother, Elizabeth, and my father, Eric, for their beliefs and values relating to education and continuous learning. To my sister Denise, I thank her for her resilience and sense of humour. To my daughter Shohreh, a personal message: *I always saw and believed in your potential*. This book is also dedicated to all the people in the world who want to lead their teams with conscious awareness, sensitivity and compassion.

Dedication by Jens Starke

Writing a book is much more difficult than I thought at the beginning of this journey in the spring of 2020. Without the motivation and support provided by my friend, mentor and co-author David, I could have lost my way more than once on the journey; so thank you for your guidance. I thoroughly enjoyed our collaboration together.

I would also like to thank my colleagues and friends, with whom I have spent many hours discussing leadership models and theories. Your curiosity towards learning and commitment to personal growth provided me with inspirational role models. Sarah, Inka and Michael, thank you for your inspiration.

But for every Yin, there is also a Yang, and therefore, a big thanks to all those who have made it clear to me why writing such a book is necessary.

My greatest appreciation, though, goes to my parents, Maritta and Gert. They have always encouraged me to go my way, to always be authentic and to never stop learning.

CONTENTS

FIGURES

TABLES

"We but mirror the world. All the tendencies present in the outer world are to be found in the world of our body. If we could change ourselves, the tendencies in the world would also change. As a man changes his own nature, so does the attitude of the world change towards him. This is the divine mystery supreme. A wonderful thing it is and the source of our happiness. We need not wait to see what others do".

Mahatma Gandhi

FOREWORD

In a decade of climate change, a global pandemic and the seemingly unstoppable spread of instability and potential conflict, it is difficult not to agree that we now need effective leadership at all levels of organisations and society more than ever. Every day the global media highlights failures of leadership and accountability and describes the consequences of self-interest coming above the needs of the nation or the company. In my experience, there are enduring aspects and principles of leadership, but leadership must also be a living thing that evolves and adapts. This is especially true in this era of rapid change, an explosion of emerging and disruptive technologies, and the inexorable rise of the importance of data and information. It is too easy to become fixated with metrics and profit at all costs and lose sight of the real objective and of our people.

This book provides an essential tool for facilitating and enabling the development of leaders and leadership. Leadership is about people and shining a light on conscious leadership, and the role of values and the impact on society is extremely timely and important. The best leaders know that they are on a constant journey of learning, and this book will be as valuable to them as it will be to emerging leaders or individuals transitioning from management to leadership. David Potter and Jens Starke have produced a methodical, understandable and compelling approach to a complex topic and offer an excellent blend of theory, academic analysis and practical advice. I have always considered trust to be a lifeblood of successful leadership, and I particularly welcome the emphasis that the book makes on communication, dialogue, engagement and emotional intelligence. It also encourages leaders to be prepared to self-examine and really take to heart notions such as leading and developing oneself to lead others and the value of improvement mechanisms such as coaching. To me, leadership has always been a 24/7 vocation rather than a job, and it is something that individuals and organisations must contently invest in. This book, and the observations and actions described, could form a key component of that investment.

A final thought is that perhaps the true test of leadership is to create the right culture of positive leadership and ethos of learning and embracement of change within a team or organisation. An important part of that undertaking is to create the conditions for enduring leadership within an organisation:

encouraging, empowering and mentoring future leaders. Conscious leadership will be key to successfully mastering that long term objective. The concept of conscious leadership may not yet be familiar to all, but it should become a foundation for the development of leaders and well-led teams. This work represents an outstanding contribution to the achievement of that goal.

Sir Graham Stacey
European Leadership Network
December 2021

INTRODUCTION

This book provides a resource to enable the emergence of leaders who aim to lead with conscious awareness to build and sustain psychologically safe cultures. The kind of team-based cultures informed by conscious leadership beliefs and values through which team members may positively engage with work in a far more meaningful and purposeful way. To help realise this ambition, this book aims to explore the dynamics of conscious leadership to enable those in leadership positions to "lead" their teams with higher levels of conscious awareness. The book is based upon the premise rooted in peer-reviewed and industrial research that a critical mass of employees is in a state of passive and active disengagement in relation to the managers expected to provide leadership in their employing organisations (Gallup, 2017). Based upon empirical research, we have established that key drivers of this disengagement are identified as a lack of psychological safety generated from very weak and underdeveloped intra- and interpersonal skills on the part of line managers (Kahn, 1990; Pech and Slade, 2006). A probable source of these weak intra- and interpersonal skills is the tendency to place emphasis on disassociated social relations with team members based on crude transactional management strategies that permeate organisational culture. This book unpacks these drivers in detail and builds a model that can be used as the basis of personal development and as a large-scale intervention into the leadership culture of an organisation. This model is very accessible and transfers to a structured training programme through a series of action learning workshops based upon coaching relationships and mutual dialogue to enable generative change in the leadership culture based on conscious leadership techniques. This is a process of personal development facilitated by reflexivity and is a practical project. The goals of the book are:

- To trigger critical reflexivity in the reader regarding their experience of leading teams and enhanced awareness of opportunities for generative change in their leadership competencies.
- To provide a practical guide, which is also theoretically informed to develop conscious leadership competencies that the reader can adopt in their day to day leadership roles.

DOI: 10.4324/9781003272793-1

- To explore and explain the underlying theory, conceptual building blocks and related body of practice of conscious leadership.
- To describe conscious leadership in a way that is both conceptually accessible and immensely practical to enable leaders to lead their teams with higher levels of conscious awareness.
- To present a model of blended leadership that can enable the crafting, with conscious awareness, of a transformation in the quality of established leadership norms.

Conscious leadership can be understood to be both a theory and practice of leadership that is rooted in literature concerning the development of conscious capitalism: a relatively new form of capitalism that advocates balancing the ambitions of an organisation with a greater social and community purpose. Its central theory is that the greater the degree of behavioural, emotional and cognitive flexibility a leader can accrue, the greater the quality of leadership relationships that will emerge.

Anderson and Anderson (2010, p. 3) explain the concept of conscious leadership as one that arguably best fits with the needs of modern change leaders. They describe conscious leaders as: "A new breed of leader for a new breed of change". They describe conscious leadership as involving: "a required shift in both leader's and consultant's consciousness regarding how they view change, themselves, and their roles as Change Leaders". The conscious leader should invest in training that aims to develop their reflective thinking capabilities as core leadership tools. In order to be effective as conscious leaders central to change work, they need to be able to critically reflect on their leadership styles, emotional choices and thinking patterns and how these are influencing their competence as a leadership practitioner. Importantly, the conscious change leader requires the ability to identify the way they are generating their perspectives and the processes they employ that delete, distort and generalise their subjective experiences.

Conscious leadership is an important shift in traditional leadership thinking. As many organisations start to identify with the notion of conscious capitalism, they need to develop a leadership culture based upon an authentic commitment to continuous personal development and thus the learning organisation. Critical to establishing positive stakeholder and staff engagement the emerging conscious leaders need to drive a corporate social responsibility agenda that makes a difference to their communities and maintain the commitment to enable all their employees access to self-actualisation opportunities. Conscious leadership is a process of internal growth that starts with the emerging leader reflecting on their emotional, behavioural and cognitive flexibility and taking responsibility for the energy they emit and how this affects the way in which their teams interact and perform.

Conscious leaders aim towards the accomplished ability to self-regulate their emotional, behavioural and cognitive states through a process of introspective reflexivity. They understand that the way in which their followers respond to them is largely influenced by their own leadership style and choices of interacting. To encourage their followers to accept their leadership style and adopt it as cultural carriers conscious leaders know that they must lead with integrity and self-awareness, authenticity and openness to personal growth and development (Potter, 2018).

Conscious leaders are very introspective. They act with acute social awareness and choose their social strategies carefully and thoughtfully. Conscious leaders are sensitive to reflecting on their social results as sources of constructive feedback. A critical competency that conscious leaders are committed to developing is the ability to evaluate their inter – and intra-personal skills and to continually aim to improve these. Conscious leaders deliberately and with awareness select their emotional, cognitive and behavioural strategies. This means that they are self-disciplined at an advanced level of meta-reflection. They look to avoid impulsive behaviors, and they make a real effort to build empathetic competencies and the skills required to understand people. Conscious leaders are involved in a process of habitually tuning inwards to meta-reflect on a social experience of importance and analysing it in terms of how productive it was. Potter (2018, p. 5) presents the following list of themes that are conscious leadership targets for meta -reflection:

- Mindset: The attitude of mind we construct based upon the way we perceive the world and the meanings we attach to our perceptions.
- Purpose: Our sense of community purpose and desire to serve and help others be the best version of themselves.
- Ego: Our sense of "I", our individualistic persona, our framework for self-validation.
- Emotions: Instinctive or intuitive feelings towards an attitude object.
- Cognitions: Our thinking patterns and preferred sensory system.
- Behaviours: The strategies we use to enact our thinking through interactions with ourselves or with others.
- Values: The scale of importance we place on a social object.
- Beliefs: The principles regarding the world and our experiences that we adhere to that we consider to be true.
- Energy transmission: Understanding the energy we are giving off and how this influences the states of individuals and groups.
- Flexibility: At an emotional, behavioural and thinking level.
- Authenticity: The ability to present one's authentic self, unfiltered.

These themes Potter (2018) claims can be described as states of being. Anderson and Anderson (2010) describe states of being as: "ways of being" and suggest that the ability to meta-reflect on one's way of being is a fundamental conscious leadership skill. They define this concept in the following way: *"Way of being is a powerful concept. It can be used to describe how leaders are 'being' and expressing themselves at any point in time or how they are relating to others in various circumstances and situations. While mindset causes emotions and behaviour, the combination is the source of a leader's way of being"* (2010, p. 169).

What is useful about the previous definition is that it implicitly points internally towards the inner sense-making dynamics of the conscious change leader.

Conscious leadership is, relative to classical leadership models and theories, a relatively new leadership model. However, it draws much of its fundamental characteristics from areas of study and practice such as organisational development, mindfulness, personal development, positive psychology and social constructivism. One could argue that conscious leadership is heavily influenced by the quest to enhance one's emotional intelligence, and we would agree with this proposition and argue that emotional intelligence is an indicator of one's standards of conscious leadership (Goleman, 2015). Conscious leadership is a merging of one's full potential to master one's emotional, cultural, behavioural, social and intellectual intelligences. Therefore, conscious leadership is always both a state of mind and a state of being underpinned by a very clear philosophy. Conscious leadership acknowledges that, as significant others in an organisation, change leaders are noticed. How change leaders behave, emote, think and decide are all expressions that people observe and react towards. Understanding the states which we bring to social encounters and the states that others may be in are important change management considerations and are central competencies for effective conscious leadership (Issah, 2018).

Core idea driving the book

It is a fundamental premise of this book that leadership starts with internal leadership; that is to say, in order to lead others, one must be able to lead oneself. This involves an introspective process of external and internal coaching. It also involves reflexivity and acute identity work on the part of the leader (Alvesson et al., 2017). It involves opening up one's mind to new ideas, new possibilities and new ways of framing past, current and future experiences that generate resourceful results for both the leader and their followers as well as key stakeholders. It is also an outward-looking body of practice which aims to build much stronger empathetic skills and relationship management skills with others. Perceptual agility is central to this element of a conscious leadership mindset. The ability to recognise when one is stuck in a closed perspective and open up one's perspective to new perspectives, which may challenge our belief system and experience, and then allow for differentiated and ultimately integrated perspectives is the basis of conscious leadership (Dixon, 1998). This book will explore conscious leadership in detail, both its theory and its body of practice. The structure for the book is as follows:

Chapter 1: Responding to the disengagement epidemic

This chapter advances the argument, based on research findings, that organisations throughout the world are experiencing a critical concentration of disengagement between staff and the managers who are expected to provide leadership. To develop a conceptual and practical appreciation of disengagement at an individual, group and intergroup level, we argue that, with conscious awareness, we can break the disengagement cycle; and we present the proposition that modelling a conscious leadership mindset and associated behavioural and emotional strategies are needed to do this.

Chapter 2: It's all about the mindset we choose

Throughout the chapter, we provide an explanation of a fixed and growth mindset drawing on the work of Dweck (2012) and connect this with personal development, and we compare the two mindsets in terms of their unique characteristics. We claim that a growth mindset and conscious leadership practices are interrelated and that people choose their mindset and, thus, should assume accountability and responsibility for their mindset of choice. Central to this chapter is the argument that conscious leadership emerges out of a growth mindset. To bring a strong sense of practicality to the ideas considered throughout this chapter, we illuminate our model of mindset becoming through a case study.

Chapter 3: Introducing leadership

In this chapter, we introduce the fundamental idea of leadership as a meta-model from which all other models of leadership are derivatives. We define leadership as involving interpersonal influencing in an asymmetrical relationship targeting meanings, feelings and values (Smircich and Morgan, 1982). All other forms of leadership prefix a noun or a verb in front of the term leadership to differentiate the derivative from others. For example, "servant" leadership and "participative" leadership, both of which are derivatives of the meta model of leadership which we present as the source of all of the derivative leadership models.

Chapter 4: Transactional and transformational leadership

In this chapter, we review transactional and transformational leadership models (Bass and Avolio, 1990). Transactional leadership, we claim, is less effective when it is based on a set of impoverished leadership/follower relationships characterised by a lack of rapport. We explore the main fault lines that are commonly associated with transactional leadership, such as: (1) management by exception passive; (2) management by exception active; and (3) personal style of the transactional leader; and review the additive effect, i.e., each of the "Four Is" that transformational leadership is based upon, e.g., idealised influence, inspirational motivation, intellectual stimulation and individualised consideration (Bass and Avolio, 1990). A fundamental idea that holds the chapter together is presented that advances the premise that both transactional and transformational leadership can be enhanced by adopting a

conscious leadership mindset and producing effective role models who demonstrate conscious leadership traits.

Chapter 5: The leadership paradox

The main argument that this chapter is making is that the idea of a model 1
mindset, as developed by Argyris and Schön (1996), and its associated leadership paradox involving the incongruence between a theory of action and a
theory in action on the part of leaders are significant drivers of disengagement
in management teams. We argue that a model 1 mindset drives disengagement; whilst again building on the work of Argyris and Schön (1996), we
argue that a model 2 mindset drives engagement and that the adoption of a
model 2 mindset is essential for the application of successful conscious leadership. Finally, we conclude with the idea that the transition from a model 1 to
a model 2 mindset is a process of gradual awakening, ideally facilitated by a
skilled conscious leadership coach.

Chapter 6: Awakening the need for change

The main aim that supports this chapter is to review and discuss the process
of conscious leadership awakening regarding the need for change based on
everyday reframing and the triggering of reflexivity (Dilts, 2003). We consider
the phenomenon of managing in the moment and how this stunts valuing
work that helps to build a future version of the organisation; we relate this to
the state of strategic myopia. Central to the challenge of awakening the case
for change is the principle that leadership style generates cultural style and
cultural style generates leadership style (Schein, 1985). Therefore, we will be
advancing the idea that transitioning through conscious leadership awakening
is a cultural change project, i.e., a wicked problem (Grint, 2008). As part of
such a cultural change project, we highlight the challenge of managing affinity
bias as a force within a leadership team for ensuring that similar management
mindsets are appointed that relate to a model 1 mindset and anti-conscious
leadership.

Chapter 7: The dynamics of anti-conscious leadership explored

In this chapter, we introduce the theory of Leadership Membership Exchange
as a resource to explore the dyadic nature of leadership relationships (Liden
et al., 2016). We also introduce the concept of anti-conscious leadership.
We discuss the theory that the principle behind Leadership Membership
Exchange (LMX) as a theory is that the leadership/follower dynamic emerges
from resourceful relationships between the leadership and follower prospects
often characterised by trust (Brower et al., 2000). We discuss the principle
that conscious leadership targets the micro interactive sense-making process,

associated behaviours and emotional expressions that affect the nature of LMX. We extend our discussion to incorporate the premise that social and cultural flexibility are fundamental, practical leadership competencies and, therefore, conscious leaders should be practising, with awareness, new behavioural, emotional and cognitive interactive strategies. The central idea is that the one-to-one dyadic relationship is where the sense-making and interactions occur that either create strong or weak leadership/followership relationships.

Chapter 8: A blended model of leadership

In this chapter, we draw inspiration from the work of Bass and Avolio (1990) to unpack our model of "blended leadership" which is a fusion of different leadership models. Our model blends the key features of: (1) transactional; (2) transformational; and (3) conscious leadership approaches. The chapter is based upon the idea that conscious leadership is the mediator that gives value and practical potential to the emergence and application of effective and high quality transactional and transformational leadership effects. Conscious leadership, we argue, can generate resourceful LMX relationships which facilitate effective transactional and transformational leadership. Initially, we explore in detail our theory of blended leadership and illustrate its main features. We propose a model of blended leadership that balances complexity with practicality and matches with the reality of leadership efforts within organisations.

Chapter 9: The dialogical conscious leader

In this chapter, we position the art of dialogue as a fundamental area of communication that the conscious leader is required to model if they are to lead with conscious awareness (Dixon, 1998). We explore, in detail, the concept of the dialogical conscious leader as a central feature of the conscious leader's identity. We emphasise dialogue because this is the main mode of communication that differentiates conscious leaders from managers and from transactional leaders. Our argument is that unless dialogical exchange is developed and practised with conscious awareness, its potential for enabling effective transformational leadership outcomes is stunted (Dixon, 1998). We relate dialogue with the process of conscious leadership awakening and as a method of self and group learning, connecting these themes with the ideas of Argyris (1990).

Chapter 10: Preparing for and actioning a dialogue seminar

Throughout this chapter, we shall discuss ways of establishing dialogical exchanges within an organisation's culture and embedding the practice of dialogue as a valued activity. An action research strategy is introduced as an awakening device in advance of a dialogue seminar. Inspired by the work of

Dixon (1998), this chapter will explore a range of dialogical techniques that a conscious leader may engage with to start facilitating the learning of conscious leadership capabilities on the part of themselves and team members. The emphasis is placed upon dialogue because, as a special kind of talk, dialogue involves diverse perspective-taking and increasing one's levels of self-awareness through quality leadership/member relationships.

Chapter 11: Conscious leadership coaching

This chapter considers the relationship between coaching and conscious leadership. As successful conscious leadership is based upon effective management and mastery of our intra- and interpersonal skills, then peer and self-coaching are both highly relevant bodies of practice for the conscious leader to learn. As conscious leaders are, at their core of existence, involved in a web of social interactions with followers, then the ability to adopt an effective coaching style contingent on the situation is a signifier of high levels of self and social awareness and conscious leadership competency. This principle equally applies to self-coaching. This chapter considers the coaching approach inspired by the client-centred methods of Carl Rogers (1957) because of their emphasis on social relationships which underpin the quality of LMX dynamics and outcomes.

Chapter 12: The emotionally intelligent conscious leader

This chapter will explore emotional intelligence as a key element of our conscious leadership model. We shall define emotional intelligence (EI) with added emphasis upon defining emotional regulation (ER) and explain its relationship with successful conscious leadership. We review key research findings to establish a conceptual base for understanding EI. We advance the idea that EI and its expressions are mainly internally generated states that drive our behaviour and interactions and, thus, have a significant influence on our social results (Goleman, 2015). Finally, we explore the process of emotional regulation as a strategy that, if practised regularly, will help develop the quality and depth of our EI as conscious leaders.

Chapter 13: Conscious leadership and psychological safety

This chapter shall consider psychological safety. as an integral element of our conscious leadership model. We review the concept of psychological safety and build a model of practice that conscious leaders may adopt to facilitate with conscious awareness the creation of a culture that supports the manifestation of psychological safety. Finally, inspired by the work of Rosabeth Moss Kanter (2013), we adopt her "Six Keys to Positive Change" and demonstrate how this model can be used in a dialogue seminar to encourage the development of psychological safety in a team.

Chapter 14: The reflexive conscious leader

This chapter reviews the final element of our conscious leadership model, reflexivity (Alvesson et al., 2017). We compare reflective practices with reflexivity and demonstrate how both methods can be used to raise our conscious awareness as leaders. The first part of this chapter builds a theoretical model of reflexivity and the second part provides examples of specific techniques that conscious leaders may use to trigger and facilitate reflexive practice. The central idea that this chapter rotates around is that reflexivity is a fundamental conscious leadership competency. Further, reflexivity involves more than reflecting upon a prior experience; it involves re-interpreting our reflective interpretations of past events and the role that our internal sense-making resources and expressive tools such as beliefs, values, ideas, vocabulary, emotions and behaviours play in generating our social results.

Chapter 15: Modelling conscious leadership

Throughout this chapter, we present our approach to modelling a conscious leadership mindset. For us, as authors, we have arrived at the conclusion that the question of "how" one transitions towards the authentic identity of a conscious leader is very important. Therefore, throughout this chapter, we address this question by drawing from the methodology of behavioural modelling (Dilts, 1998). This chapter leaves you, the reader, with one big idea: conscious leadership is a state of being in the world that can be modelled by applying practical methods. To be a conscious leader is a continual process of being a conscious leader, of modelling the characteristics and traits of a conscious leader. It has a philosophy that underpins the decisions we make in all aspects of our interactions with ourselves and with others and involves lifetime learning.

Chapter 16: Building a culture of conscious leadership

Our final chapter pulls on key themes that underpin elements of the preceding chapters to provide an outline strategy regarding how one would approach the task of building a conscious leadership culture. We start with the task of framing organisational culture and then defining cultural change work. The idea that stakeholder engagement and leadership capabilities should be embedded into the corporate governance of the organisation and risk assessed yearly is then introduced. We examine the process of awakening the need for change in leadership styles. The role of dialogue seminars as key technology to support the case for change is emphasised once more. We then re-visit coaching as an enabler for cultural change. We conclude with the argument that the potential success of this cultural change process would be dependent on the active and present role modelling of a conscious leadership mindset throughout the leadership network within an organisation.

References

Alvesson, M., Blok, M. & Sveningsson, S. (2017) *Reflexive Leadership: Organising in an Imperfect World*. Sage.

Anderson, D. & Anderson, L. (2010) *Beyond Change Management: How to Achieve Breakthrough Results Through Conscious Change Leadership*. John Wiley and Sons.

Argyris, C. (1990) *Overcoming Organizational Defenses*. Prentice-Hall.

Argyris, C. & Schön, D.A. (1996) *Organizational Learning II: Theory, Method and Practice*. Addison Wesley.

Bass, B.M. & Avolio, B.J. (1990) The Implications of Transactional and Transformational Leadership for Individual, Team, and Organizational Development. *Research in Organizational Change and Development*, 4, pp 231–72.

Brower, H., Schoorman, F.D. & Tan, H.H. (2000) A Model of Relational Leadership: The Integration of Trust and Leader – Member Exchange. *The Leadership Quarterly*, 11, pp. 227–250.

Dilts, R. (1998) *Modelling with NLP*. Meta Publications.

Dilts, R. (2003) *From Coach to Awakener*. Meta Publications.

Dixon, N.M. (1998) *Dialogue at Work*. Lemos & Crane.

Dweck, C.S. (2012) *Mindset: How You Can Fulfil Your Potential*. Constable & Robinson.

Gallup (2017) *State of the Global Work Place – Gallup Report*. Gallup Press.

Goleman, D. (2015) *Emotional Intelligence*. Vietnam Labor Publishing House.

Grint, K. (2008) Wicked Problems and Clumsy Solutions: The Role of Leadership. *Clinical Leader*, 1, 11.

Issah, M. (2018) *Change Leadership: The Role of Emotional Intelligence*. Sage Open.

Kahn, W.A. (1990) Psychological Conditions of Personal Engagement and Disengagement at Work. *Academy of Management Journal*, 33, pp. 692–724.

Kanter, M.R. (2013) *Six Keys to Positive Change*. Ted Talk. https://conorneill.com/2016/07/06/6-keys-to-leading-positive-change-rosabeth-moss-kanter/.

Liden, R., Anand, S. & Vidyarthi, P. (2016) Dyadic Relationships. *Annual Review of Organizational Psychology and Organizational Behavior*, 3(10), p. 1146.

Pech, R. & Slade, B. (2006) Employee Disengagement: Is There Evidence of a Growing Problem? *Handbook of Business Strategy*, 7, pp. 21–25.

Potter, D. (2018) *Neuro-Linguistic Programming for Change Leaders: The Butterfly Effect*. Routledge.

Rogers, C.R. (1957) The Necessary and Sufficient Conditions of Therapeutic Personality Change. *Journal of Consulting Psychology*, 21(2), pp. 95–103.

Schein, H.E. (1985) *Organisational Culture and Leadership*. Jossey-Bass.

Smircich, L. & Morgan, G. (1982) Leadership: The Management of Meaning. *Journal of Applied Behavioural Science*, 18, pp. 257–273.

1 RESPONDING TO THE DISENGAGEMENT EPIDEMIC

Introduction

This chapter reviews the important organisational issue of disengagement. We illuminate the significant challenge facing organisations in relation to building an engaged workforce in the face of a disengagement epidemic that is plaguing organisations worldwide. There are many different reasons why employees may find themselves either passively or actively disengaged. We will not review literature concerned with workload, work-life issues or negative stress as this literature has been more than adequately covered. Rather, we focus in on the function of leaders influencing the shaping of employee mindsets to enable the internalisation of an engaged state (Pink, 2017). As important, though, we also emphasise the nature of disengagement and its drivers from the perspective of social and psychological resources – or lack thereof. Drawing upon the COACH and CRASH state models as developed by behavioural change experts Robert Dilts and Stephen Gilligan we offer a reconceptualisation of staff disengagement and engagement to the expression, or lack of expression, of a conscious leader's mindset.

Why disengagement matters

In the Gallup State of the World Workplace Report (2017, p. 5), the research team make the following claims:

> Worldwide, the percentage of adults who work full time for an employer and are engaged at work – they are highly involved in and enthusiastic about their work and workplace – is just 15%. That low percentage of engaged employees is a barrier to creating high-performing cultures. It implies a stunning amount of wasted potential, given that business units in the top quartile of our global employee engagement database are 17% more productive and 21% more profitable than those in the bottom quartile.

DOI: 10.4324/9781003272793-2

The Gallup report research findings are reflected in the work of Rastogi et al. (2018), who estimate, from various research sources, that in excess of 70% of the workforce is either passively or actively disengaged. These are incredibly worrying statistics; only three out of ten employees are positively engaged with their work and its vision and ambitions. It is estimated by Gallup researchers that the economic cost of this global disengagement epidemic can be estimated at approximately $7 trillion in lost productivity. The effects of employee disengagement on organisational effectiveness are well established (Rastogi et al., 2018) and include variables such as:

- Diminished employee morale and productivity.
- Enhanced employee turnover and accidents.
- Losses to the organisation and economy.
- Lack of staff commitment.
- Increased turnover intention.
- Low energy and lack of social vitality.
- Social withdrawal disconnection.
- General dissatisfaction with the organisation.
- Poor work performance.
- Counterproductive work behaviours.

A common finding is that disengaged employees are often in dissociated states in relation to their work and their supposed leaders and have been described in the following metaphoric terms as being *"checked-out"* (Zenger and Folkman, 2014) and *"going through the motions"* (Pater, 2013). In even more colourful terms, researchers such as Singh (2009, p. 22) state that disengaged staff: "Leave the best of their heart, mind and spirit elsewhere when they show up at work". A lack of trust between staff and their potential leaders is a significant contributor towards employee disengagement (Brower et al., 2000).

Jim Harter, PhD, Chief Scientist, Workplace Management and Wellbeing at Gallup, puts forward the convincing hypothesis that: "This global engagement pattern provides evidence that how performance is managed, and specifically how people are being developed, is misfiring" (Harter, 2017). The traditional model of the transactional benevolent manager is being rejected in favour of a desire to engage with a coach and mentor (Herminia and Scoular, 2019). Scholars such as Imperatori (2017) call for a reframing of the organisation-employee relationship, noting solemnly that traditionally trained managers often lack the behavioural and relational flexibility to operate effectively as leaders. The new generation of employees is responding to managers who lean towards coaching and mentoring and who emphasise the strengths of the team member rather than obsessing over weaknesses. Imperatori (2017, p. 18) sums up this dilemma when she claims that: "Today, managers need to be more aware of the employees' needs, motivation drivers, expectation and emotions, because they need to activate their energy despite uncertainty, growing responsibility, time pressure, diversity and ambiguity". This may be interpreted as a call for the development of conscious leadership skills, i.e., to lead with awareness, and this journey of personal development will not be easy for a generation of managers who have been raised on a diet of command and control and transactional leadership strategies as influencing resources. Imperatori (2017, p. 18) acknowledges this when she states that: "The managerial function therefore needs to change: The human and relational sides of management behaviours are now compulsory to manage growing organizational complexity and help employees enact sense-making. This is a big challenge, but it is also a big chance". Thus, to reverse the global trend from one of staff disengagement to one of a predominant staff engagement culture in the global workplace, we need to rethink how managers manage and how leaders lead with awareness and sensitivity regarding their beliefs, values and related behavioural, cognitive and emotional strategies that underpin their approach and relationships with potential followers. The common theme that runs through much of the research into the causes of staff disengagement is a lack of resources at work to enable employees to build positive identities at an individual, group and organisational level.

Defining engagement and disengagement through identity theory

Kahn (1990, pp. 700–701) defines personal engagement as involving: "The simultaneous employment and expression of a person's 'preferred self' in task behaviours that promote connections to work and to others, personal presence (physical, cognitive, and emotional), and active, full role performances", and he contrasts this with his definition of disengagement which is defined as: "The simultaneous withdrawal and defence of a person's preferred self in behaviours that promote a lack of connections, physical, cognitive, and emotional absence, and passive, incomplete role performances". Crucially, Kahn locates as central to both definitions the concept of self, thus indicating identity as a key aspect of both states, i.e., disengaged and engaged. It is important that we do not nominalise the states of being disengaged and engaged as these are processes that we engage with; they are not fixed entities, they are processes of sense-making and, as such, they are both open to transformative change. Kahn (1990) underscores the self-concept with the idea of a "preferred self".

The concept of a preferred self denotes an identity construct that we create and internalise as our best version of ourselves when at work. This is the version of one's self who comes to work with positive intentions and seeks outlets to self-actualise and contribute in a meaningful way to work. One could argue that the role of the conscious leader is to elicit the free, unconstrained expression of our preferred self at work. Kahn (1990) identifies that, for the preferred self to emerge productively, the person must experience strong feelings of psychological safety, psychological meaningfulness and psychological availability.

We explore the concept of psychological safety and its relationship with conscious leadership in depth throughout Chapter 13. However, at this juncture, a brief definition is necessary. Edmondson (1999, p. 6) defines psychological safety as: "A shared belief that the team is safe for interpersonal risk taking. In psychologically safe teams, team members feel accepted and respected".

A crucial psychological condition for full engagement with one's work is psychological availability which involves having confidence in one's abilities and status, thus enabling: "A focus on tasks rather than anxieties" (Kahn, 1990, p. 716). Kahn (1990, p. 700) defines psychological availability as: "The sense of having the physical, emotional, or psychological resources to personally engage at a particular moment". Another way to think about psychological availability is the idea of being fully present and engaged. Finally, psychological meaningfulness can be defined as: "Feeling that one is receiving a return on investments of one's self in a currency of physical, cognitive, or emotional energy" (Kahn, 1990, p. 704). This is important as a common fault line running through impoverished models of transactional leadership is a tick box mentality towards the work people do. If the emphasis is on task completion in return for financial reward, then the depth of engagement will potentially be diluted on the part of the worker in relation to the work. Human beings need to feel recognised and appreciated, and in the absence of such emotional states, they will most probably disengage. Therefore, it is incumbent on the leader to value the work and the worker's role in the work process and to recognise their contribution (Maslow, 1954; McGregor, 1960; Rogers, 1961).

Kahn (1990) draws our attention to the idea of being "present" as a central characteristic of an engaged state. To be present involves bringing your whole sense of preferred self to an encounter. Opening your mind to others' perspectives, suspending judgmentalism and presenting a curious mindset. This involves giving one's full attention to one's companions and engaging in active listening. To be present is to be connected, open, attentive, relaxed and centred (Dilts, 2017). In contrast, when in a disengaged state, one withdraws and maintains a contracted state of active or passive separation from the attitude object. When in a disengaged state, Kahn (1990) refers to behaviours that generate dissociated relationships, at the level of behaviours, emotions and cognitions, and superficial passive performance at work. In doing so, he is drawing our attention to the concept of being emotionally absent, which is the polar opposite to being present. A major source of disengagement and engagement catalysts emanates from the mindset and associated behavioural, emotional and cognitive states adopted on the part of line managers who have an expectancy that they will generate leadership as an integral aspect of their job role.

Leaders influence mindset choices

It is a central proposition of this book that the state of the leader's mindset functions as a significant catalyst for driving staff engagement or disengagement at work (Kahn, 1990). For work to be interpreted as psychologically meaningful, the leader and their potential followers must co-author the purpose, mission, vision and ambition of the organisation and align these variable concepts with the individual. It is crucial that the leader understands the psychological resources their followers need and coaches them implicitly or explicitly to create the internal: "Sense of having the physical, emotional, or psychological resources to personally engage during a particular moment" (Kahn, 1990, p. 714).

In summary, psychological availability is a belief that staff can present themselves authentically at work. Also, it is important to acknowledge the function of sense-making as a fundamental element of the engagement and disengagement process (Ayla et al., 2016). It is established that how we frame our experiences will have a significant influence on our state of engagement or disengagement at work. This process can be referred to as "everyday reframing", a process through which we may change the meanings we attach to an experience and, thus, change our identity position towards an attitude object. Alvesson (2008) suggests that everyday reframing involves interpreting and re-interpreting sense data and framing perceptions of experience with specific content embedded in a specific context. We know that significant others, such as leaders, can have a powerful influence on this sense-making process. For scholars such as Alvesson (2008), leadership is primarily concerned with "meaning-making".

Identity work

We can think of engaged staff as being psychologically present, attentive to what's going on, curious, energised and fully absorbed in what they are doing at work and deriving a strong sense of social identity from their work. Identity work has increasingly developed as a focus of enquiry for many scholars and is seen as a critical aspect of organisational change management competency (Beech and MacIntosh, 2012). The reasons that people may or may not engage with an organisation will always be varied. However, the identity position, e.g., positive or negative, they adopt in relation to their potential leaders is an important consideration (Elsbach, 1999). Different expressions of identity work as resources connected with organisational performance are long established within behavioural science literature.

The process of disengagement

Due to cultural norms, the nature of identity positions will be influenced by the culture of an organisation. Myriad factors can impact the identity position that both individuals and groups adopt. Disengaged staff often experience states of feeling contracted from their work identity resources such as their potential leader, co-workers, organisational mission and ambitions, as well as their job role. By contraction, we mean that the individual may deliberately minimise the status of their presence, expressive capacity, availability and commitment to an aspect of their organisational experience, for example, their line manager as a potential leader.

They may experience acute emotional reactions stimulated by habitual reactions to internal or external stimuli. For example, the person may feel that a manager talked over them and perceived it as an insult. This would generate an emotional response based on this interpretation that may be disturbing. They may discuss this event with others and, thus, re-live the experience internally and, again, react emotionally in a way that is upsetting for them. This reactive process is a serious disengagement catalyst. Disengagement catalysts can be understood as any experience of an event that is perceived to threaten the socially desirable sense of self that a person has internalised as a valued asset.

Staff in a disengaged state may also be overly analytical in relation to events that threaten their sense of self. They can become stuck in a frame of reference that they continually re-analyse, thus reverting back to the triggering of negative emotional responses. The habitualisation of reacting generated by repetitive analysis will not only generate emotional responses, but it will also generate somatic responses, i.e., physiological manifested states that become anchors in themselves for the attitude object that initially triggered the contraction, reaction and habitual analysis. This can be understood as a process of internal conditioning.

CRASH state

The dominant state that is associated with disengaged staff is one of separation. Disengaged staff often feel separate from their line managers and their organisation's mission, vision and ambitions. They can feel separate from co-workers and even separate from their actual job role. When in this acute and multi-dimensional state of separation, staff can experience very low levels of energy and morale, and they may also be in a highly dissociated state. They will be hurting, experiencing an emotional pain, and this hurt is like a toothache, it simply wears the individual down. We call this super negative state CRASH state, a model that was developed by Californian based behavioural change experts Robert Dilts, Deborah Bacon Dilts and Stephen Gilligan.

CRASH state explained

CRASH state is an expression of what could be called a super-toxic state of disengagement manifesting as a mindset. When trying to understand staff disengagement, we can adopt the strategy of coming to the problem through the resource of identity work using the CRASH state model as an analytical tool to unpack the disengagement catalysts that are driving the CRASH state mindset literally into the neurological and physiological systems of the disengaged staff. The acronym CRASH state represents the following states:

Contracted: Feelings of lack of connection with the organisation and one's colleagues.

Reactive: Not having time to reflect and being led by one's emotions.

Analysis paralysis: Continually replaying events over and over in one's mind and building toxic emotions.

Separate: Feeling alone and lacking in trusting relationships within the workplace.

Hurting: Feeling undervalued, underwhelmed, regretting not having the chance to really make a difference at work.

Modelling CRASH state

An important consideration is what happens if the person who is supposed to be generating leadership is, themselves, in CRASH state. This is a significant problem for organisations. People who are in leadership positions can be regarded as significant others and, as such, potential role models (Mead, 1934). If they are in CRASH state, they will most certainly be experiencing disengagement and spreading disengagement catalysts through intuitive modelling (Dilts, 1998) and through what Hatfield et al. (1994, p. 5) refer to as emotional contagions, which the authors define as: "The tendency to automatically mimic and synchronize facial expressions, vocalizations, postures, and movements with those of another person's and, consequently, to converge emotionally". Emotional contagions can be understood by the simple example of when we watch a sports event with two teams competing. When one team scores, all the supporting fans applaud and reach emotional states that are ecstatic, and, in contrast, the away fans drop their energy levels and groan in unison. Thus, we adopt the emotions and related behaviours of our colleagues; we literally model our colleagues' emotional mindsets and states of being.

Emotional contagions and secondary gains

The main symptoms of the CRASH state are the emotional and related behavioural states that are generated, such as overt dominance, aggression, anxiety, fear, anger, low tolerance, irritation and sadness. These emotional states and their associated behaviours can become culturally acceptable. They become ingrained within the cultural DNA of the organisation. This happens, despite its harmful effects because: (1) emotional states are contagious; and (2) the person modelling these states derives a secondary gain from internalising a toxic emotion related to the CRASH state that is not healthy for their happiness; they get stuck in the CRASH state. Secondary gains are the benefits that people derive from maintaining a state that is arguably harmful to them. For example, a potential leader might maintain the CRASH state and its associated emotions because it means that they do not have to step up as a leader; they may fear being rejected by potential followers.

Thus, it is incumbent upon the emerging leader to critically reflect on their emotional, cognitive and behavioural states and adjust these if they find themselves stuck in the CRASH state, which is a significant disengagement catalyst. If the leader, or their team, is in the CRASH state, in total or in part, this is a major barrier to collaborative working and generating commitment. The task of the leader is to help the team member shift their state towards the COACH state that involves far more resourceful mindsets, which was also developed by Robert Dilts, Deborah Bacon Dilts and Stephen Gilligan.

COACH state

COACH state is a "super-resourceful" mindset that enables high performance, conscious leadership; the acronym COACH can be understood as follows:

Centred: You develop a sense of being fully centred and strong as you become more aware that the roots that give you strength are vividly brought to life.

Open: Your mind is opened more fully to new ideas, perspectives and alternative cultures and their life philosophies, stimulating you and enriching your perceptual map, giving you more choices in life.

Attentive/aware: You fully experience being aware of, and attentive to, your own needs and the needs of colleagues.

Connected: You experience a high level of connection with colleagues.

Holding: You are able to hold challenging emotions such as stress or anxiety and make them work for you productively.

A fundamental aspect of conscious leadership is being able to self-calibrate one's state and manage this accordingly. Thus, the challenge of the conscious leader is to elicit the COACH state in themselves and in their audience. This is especially important as a conscious leader, as many management cultures are in the CRASH state and simply don't know how to transform this unproductive state of mind and enjoy far more productive team-based relationships. As conscious leaders, we can calibrate the strength of our COACH states by conducting a COACH state audit which simply involves critically reflecting on one's state of mind by asking oneself the following questions:

Centred: Do I feel secure in this situation and can I rely on my ability to fit in?

Open: Do I feel open to the ideas of others, curious and secure in being open about my own thoughts?

Attentive: Am I attentive to the needs of my colleagues?

Connected: Do I feel connected to my team?

Holding: Can I recognise my emotional states, and can I hold on to them in a resourceful way?

This is a safe technique that presents no threat to the public version of the conscious leader, and it's a technique that is easily modelled and self-administered. You can programme your mind to adopt a mindset that privileges COACH state orientations as a conscious leader. This involves building your COACH state.

Conclusion

A fundamental responsibility of the role as a conscious leader is to generate an environment within which people can feel confident in their relationship with the leader as a highly influential person so that they may express themselves without fear of any attack on their sense of self. Therefore, a meeting room is no longer a meeting room; instead, it is to be understood as a creative space through which difficult feelings may be held and channelled safely. This is a style of leadership that involves building a relationship through which we, as the lead influencers, act as caretakers of the environment that our audience is to operate within during their interactions with us (Dilts, 2003). This involves accepting our responsibility to lead the others into a COACH state, within which they feel no threat to their established identities. This involves providing a safe and supportive environment. At its heart, conscious leadership is concerned with the intra- and interpersonal skills required to generate engagement catalysts. The next chapter will consider the role of mindset in working with these building blocks productively and with conscious awareness.

References

Alvesson, M. (2008) The Construction of Organizational Identity: Comparative Case Studies of Consulting Firms. *Scandinavian Journal of Management*, 24(1).

Ayla, E. & Dizdar, A.O. (2016) Sensemaking at Work: Meaningful Work Experience for Individuals and Organizations. *International Journal of Organizational Analysis*, 24, pp. 2–17.

Beech, N. & MacIntosh, R. (2012) *Managing Change Enquiry and Action*. Cambridge University Press.

Brower, H., Schoorman, F.D. & Tan, H.H. (2000) A Model of Relational Leadership: The Integration of Trust and Leader – Member Exchange. *The Leadership Quarterly*, 11, pp. 227–250.

Dilts, R. (1998) *Modelling with NLP*. Meta Publications.

Dilts, R. (2003) *From Coach to Awakener*. Meta Publications.

Dilts, R. (2017) *Conscious Leadership and Resilience*. Dilts Strategy Group.

Edmondson, A. (1999) Psychological Safety and Learning Behavior in Work Teams. *Administrative Science Quarterly*, 44(2), pp. 350–383.

Elsbach, D. (1999) An Expanded Model of Organizational Identification. *Research in Organizational Behaviour*, 21, pp. 13–200.

Gallup State of the World Workplace Report (2017) https://www.slideshare.net/adrian-boucek/state-of-the-global-workplace-gallup-report-2017#:~:text=Only%20 15%25%20of%20employees%20worldwide,staggering%20waste%20of%20 human%20potential.

Harter, J. (2017) *Dismal Employee Engagement Is a Sign of Global Mismanagement*. www.gallup.com/workplace/231668/dismal-employee-engagement-sign-global-mis-management.aspx.

Hatfield, E., Cacioppo, J. & Rapson, R.L. (1994) *Emotional Contagion*. Cambridge University Press.

Herminia, I. & Scoular, A. (2019) The Leader as Coach. *Harvard Business Review*.

Imperatori, B. (2017) "Engagement and Disengagement at Work: What's New" Springer Briefs in Business. In: *Engagement and Disengagement at Work*. Springer, pp. 5–18.

Kahn, W.A. (1990) Psychological Conditions of Personal Engagement and Disengagement at Work. *Academy of Management Journal*, 33, pp. 692–724.

Maslow, H.A. (1954) *Motivation and Personality*, 3rd edn. Addison Wesley.

McGregor, D. (1960) *The Human Side of Enterprise*. McGraw-Hill, Maidenhead.

Mead, H.G. (1934) *Mind, Self and Society, from the Stand Point of a Social Behaviourist*. University of Chicago Press.

Pater, R. (2013) Keen-Sighted Leadership for Cultural Change. *Professional Safety*, 58(1), Article 24.

Pink, D. (2017) *Drive: The Surprising Truth About What Motivates Us*. Cannon Gate.

Rastogi, A., Pati, S.P., Krishnan, T.N. & Krishnan, S. (2018) Causes, Contingencies, and Consequences of Disengagement at Work: An Integrative Literature Review. *Human Resource Development Review*, 17(1), pp. 62–94.

Rogers, C.R. (1961) *On Becoming a Person*. Houghton Mifflin.

Singh, J. (2009, February). Leveraging Your Talent for Superior Performance. *Human Resource Magazine*, pp. 22–23.

Zenger, J. & Folkman, J. (2014) Your Employees Want the Negative Feedback You Hate to Give. *Harvard Business Review*.

2 IT'S ALL ABOUT THE MINDSET WE CHOOSE

Introduction

This chapter builds the case for considering leadership as an influencing process which is heavily dependent on the mindset that the potential leader develops. We borrow from the work of Carol Dweck (2012) who has pioneered research into the role and influence that mindset plays in learning and development. We extend the conceptual models that she develops in relation to learning to the subject of leadership, especially conscious leadership and its effects. The basic premise of Dweck's work is that human beings have a choice in relation to mindset in that they may choose a fixed or growth mindset. This choice, Dweck argues, influences the capacity for learning and personal growth on the part of the individual. Our main aim throughout this chapter is to advance the premise that conscious leadership can be enabled from the perspective of a growth mindset on the part of the leader.

As authors, we assume that Dweck intended her model of growth and fixed mindsets to be metaphors for the attitude we adopt towards a learning and self-development opportunity. In this sense, a fixed or growth mindset implies a state of mind based on core beliefs and values and life experiences as opposed to a biological and physiological part of the brain. Our fundamental argument is that potential conscious leaders must be able to identify when they are gravitating towards a fixed mindset, or when they may be habitually stuck in a fixed mindset that is hindering their leadership potential. We consider the role that our life experience, beliefs and values play in influencing our mindset of choice and the practical advantages of instilling mindful reflective techniques to help leaders manage their mindset choices with greater flexibility of awareness.

Conceptualising fixed and growth mindsets

Dweck (2012) defines mindset as a form of self-theory that a person has internalised about themselves. She illustrates this idea with the contrasting belief that two people may hold regarding their intelligence, e.g., one may have a

DOI: 10.4324/9781003272793-3

mindset that claims that they are intelligent whilst the other, in contrast, may hold the theory of self that claims that they are not intelligent. Another example from our own experience as consultant trainers is that one person may believe that they do not have leadership capabilities whilst another may, again, in contrast, believe that they do have leadership capabilities. In fact, in both examples, it may well be the case that both are equally intelligent and both have leadership potential; however, the mindset that we have internalised as our self-theory may influence the choices we make in life, and thus, our social results. One person applies for leadership positions and the other does not; one person applies to complete an MBA and the other does not. These decisions we make, based on our mindset, will influence our careers.

Keating et al. (2015, p. 331), influenced by Dweck's ideas, consider mindsets as a: "mental framework that guide how people think, feel, and act in achievement contexts". This idea implies that our mindset acts as a compass, as a navigator that guides us through our social experiences. Our mindset probably also operates through the medium of confirmation bias in that it selects evidence that confirms the core beliefs that underpin it. Confirmation bias is defined by Nickerson (1998, p. 175) as: "Confirmation bias, as the term is typically used in the psychological literature, connotes the seeking or interpreting of evidence in ways that are partial to existing beliefs, expectations, or a hypothesis in hand". Regardless of whether one holds a fixed or growth mindset regarding personal growth and development, our confirmation bias will constantly be surveying our experiences and framing these to support our beliefs. Thus, a conscious leader needs to be able to identify the nature of their unconscious bias and understand its antecedents and, if required, reframe these.

Keating et al. (2015, p. 331) also make the case that mindsets are: "the implicit theories or assumptions that people hold about the plasticity of their abilities". This implies that our current mindset has antecedents; it has a personal history. Our mindset is forged from our social experience which is a social construction. For each event we experience, we attribute meaning to that event, and this meaning attribution is based upon and freezes our beliefs and our values. Our beliefs and values fuse together to form our personal theories of our self-identity, our potential for growth and our place in the world and how we relate to others. If we have an experience as a child that we interpret as evidence that we can develop our skills, that we are good at learning and that our point of view is welcomed, then this formative experience may morph into enabling beliefs that we have a capacity and a joy for learning. In contrast, if we have a formative childhood experience that we are not good learners, that we should simply do what we need to pass the tests and no more and that we are to be seen and not heard in the classroom, then this experience may form into limiting beliefs about our identity as learners and our relationship with learning opportunities.

Another important aspect of mindsets is that, often, we are unaware that we hold these. They may operate below the level of conscious thought yet still have a powerful grip on our decision-making. Dweck (2012) extended the idea of mindset to include two apparently asymmetrical concepts: fixed and growth mindsets. According to Dweck, in a fixed mindset, people believe their abilities, like their intelligence or leadership potential, are fixed traits, thus, implicitly assuming the case of nature over nurture. In contrast, people with a growth mindset believe that their personality and capabilities can grow and develop subject to applied study and learning, implicitly assuming nurture over nature.

Importantly, we do not argue that fixed and growth mindsets are general attitudes dominating all learning opportunities; rather, they are contingent on both situational context and subject content. This means that we acknowledge that a person can, at times, hold a fixed or a growth mindset; it is not the case that they hold an exclusive fixed or growth mindset though they may orientate towards one over the other as a general intrapersonal coping strategy. So, our mindset is not always programmed towards fixed or growth, it can be plastic and contingent on context; for example, a manager or executive may not believe that leadership is relevant in a business organisation, that it requires too much investment and can detract from the day-to-day functions of management. However, they may paradoxically believe that, in the military, leadership is a fundamental competitive competency that does require intensive investment and daily practice and education.

Historical antecedents of mindset

How we frame experiences as infants, adolescents, teenagers and adults influences the development and reinforcement of our mindset of choice. However, it is important to remember that we must not nominalise the concept of mindset, i.e., turn what is a process of becoming, and therefore a verb, into a fixed entity that is part of us, e.g., a noun. Our mindset has a history; it has a developmental timeline that is part of our personal history. Therefore, to change aspects of our mindset does require reframing aspects of how we have framed the content and context of events within our timeline and, thus, changing how we have socially interpreted our personal history (Dilts, 2018).

Framing as a concept is based upon the theory of social constructivism and explains the way in which people socially construct their culture to interact successfully. The process of social construction through which we generate our interpretive frames is incredibly complex and beyond the scope of this book to explain, however the basic principles are easily grasped. We all filter our experiences through our beliefs, values and attitudes and we then rearrange our daily experiences as frames of reference that we store in our memories. These frames of reference that we socially construct are often validated through our interaction with our peers.

We socially interact with others based on the meanings that these socially constructed frames of reference mean to us. These socially interactive processes thus generate our social results. This means that how we frame experience can be correlated with the social results we experience through our

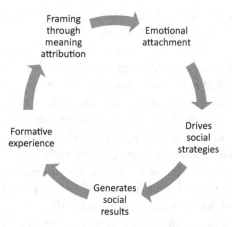

Figure 2.1 Mindset Framing Cycle

interactions. This implies that if we are open to critically reflecting on the utility of our interpretive frames we can adjust or even transform these to generate new social outcomes. The framing cycle model (Figure 2.1) explains the framing and sense-making process that generates our mindsets.

Whenever we have a formative experience, a social event, we frame this by attaching meaning to the event in relation to both content and context. Depending on the importance of this event to us, we apply an intensity of emotional attachment to the formative experience. This emotional attachment influences our choice of social strategies (behaviours, decisions and attitudes), which generate our social results. Then, when we once again experience the event or a similar event, it serves as an anchor to the formative experience, which triggers the cycle we have imprinted on our mind. The habitualisation of the cycle generates our mindset and is an example of classic conditioning (Grimley, 2019).

This kind of framing of experience has limiting effects not only on the person doing the framing but also, perhaps, on others who are influenced by this person. If we can critically reflect on our framed experience in terms of its content, context and function, then we can intervene and socially reconstruct our frames of reference, change our associated attitudes and generated behavioural strategies and, thus, change the nature of our mindsets. This process is called "reframing", which is defined by O'Connor and Seymour (2011, p. 234) as: "Changing the frame of reference around a statement or an event to give it another meaning". Reframing is a coaching resource application that can transform the experience of individuals and groups. In the reframing model (Figure 2.2), we can see that reframing the formative experience will generate a new emotional attachment and state, thus driving alternative social strategies and generating different social results. This reframing process can, and often does, lead to a change in mindset.

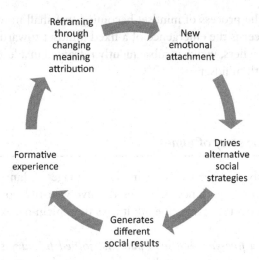

Figure 2.2 Reframing Process

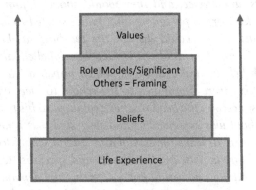

Figure 2.3 The Unconscious Mindset Conditioning Model

Reframing is both deeply introspective and reflexive. It is a process that, initially, one can experiment with using one's internal coach. This idea of an internal coach is integral to the state of being we call conscious leadership and will be further developed throughout this book. The main point we are developing is that our mindset of choice is a social construction, our personal social construction, and, thus, is always open to reconstruction and change.

Mindset as a social construction

We know that mindset as a social construct is historically formed. One way to explain this mindset becoming process is by analysing its developmental journey through the interplay between all four layers of "The Unconscious Mindset Conditioning Model" presented below (Figure 2.3).

To elucidate the process of mindset becoming, we shall now review a case study which concerns the emergence of a fixed mindset towards learning and the framing of teachers, which is subsequently reframed in adulthood, fuelling a powerful growth mindset.

Case study: the story of James

This case study has been crafted in the language of James the adult reflecting on the experience of James the five-year-old boy and, thus, employs concepts that James the adult uses to explain his experience as a five-year-old.

James was a five-year-old who had just joined primary school. This was his first experience of teachers and organised structured learning. James was a very energetic boy who loved being the centre of attention. He would constantly ask questions and speak up during class which was to his teachers' annoyance, and they would shout at James and order him to stop talking or simply ignore him. James started to look for other forms of attention and would disrupt the teachings as he interacted, often playfully, with other children. The teachers labelled James a disruptive child with behavioural challenges, which impeded learning. James' mother and father were summoned to the school to meet with the head teacher. At this meeting, the head teacher explained to his parents the difficulties the school was experiencing and suggested that it would be best for James if he were to leave the school and enter a school for intellectually challenged pupils with smaller classes and specialist teaching staff. James' parents did not and would not accept this and demanded a second opinion. So James spent time with a child psychiatrist who determined after some tests that James was, in fact, entirely normal and had the clear potential to learn and develop and would, given time and thoughtful teaching, settle down into the school system and probably flourish academically.

James framed this formative experience by adopting a fixed mindset towards his ability to learn and his relationship towards teachers. His fixed mindset was based on the hugely limiting belief that he was not the kind of person that teachers wanted in their classrooms. He also believed that teachers were authority figures who were to be challenged and/or avoided. Although a five-year-old, he understood the rejection he was experiencing and so continued to rebel and avoid any form of productive learning relationship with his teachers. This trend continued beyond primary and into secondary school. Eventually, James left school at 14, which was two years before the legal age for leaving school, and he left without any formal academic qualifications.

James' parents were skilled tradespersons who admired and valued both vocational and academic education. His father believed in his potential and would often challenge James to learn and apply himself. His father would tell James that when he was ready to embrace study, he would excel and could achieve whatever he wanted to in academic and professional terms.

His father, when James was around 14 and he was in his mid-40s, committed himself to a course of distance learning over three years to achieve a diploma in Building Estimation, which would enable him to move from a trade role to a white-collar professional role with more money and a larger pension. James used to watch his father studying late into the night with complicated algebra, physics and engineering equations and models. His father passed all his exams and qualified and achieved his goals for promotion and started a new career in his late 40s.

James positively identified with the role model his father presented. He decided later in life to re-sit his school-level qualifications at night school, and he passed them all. He enjoyed a flourishing career in management, reaching senior management level within the Public Sector. He completed an Executive MBA and a PhD at one of the United Kingdom's leading business schools. Now he teaches in prominent universities on master's degree programmes and develops both face-to-face and online academic courses. The catalyst for his transformation from a fixed to a growth mindset in relation to his relationship with teachers/educators and his ability to fit into a learning institution and flourish was the value that his father placed upon education and hard work. James had internalised his father's belief and value system, and this had, like a seed, germinated inside of him so that through time he reframed his personal history and adopted a powerful growth mindset towards personal development.

We can see from the analysis of the above that mindset, be it fixed or growth, in relation to an attitude object, in this case interacting productively with teachers and personal learning, are not intrinsic aspects of our personality. They are social constructions, and their foundations always lie within our content and context framing of our beliefs of the formative experiences that generated the belief.

Recurring theme

The theme that runs through the above example is that we cannot disconnect our past from our present if we want to reflect upon and unpack the antecedents that forged our mindset of choice (Dweck, 2012). Our mindset has a history, and only by acknowledging this history can we truly understand the social forces that have shaped it, which continue to mould ourselves and our personalities. To change the form of our mindset relative to a given situation, we need to move back down our timeline to the beginning of its genesis and then reframe the meanings we attached to either the content or context, or both, of the events in our life experience which acted as the catalysts for shaping our mindset (James, 2017). This idea also has additional and profound implications; it means that many of us as adults, and as professionals, are applying mindsets based upon values and beliefs that were forged when we were children.

Our personalities are not fixed; they are aspects of ourselves that are always open to change. Our mindset is always a projection of our personality, and conscious leaders understand that they are all work in motion. They can, if they choose to, intervene internally and reflect upon the way they are framing their experiences and how these frames influence their emotional states, interactions with others and behaviours (O'Connor and Seymour, 2011). We can think of our emotional states, behavioural states and thinking states as "strategies". This reframe is helpful because if we accept as conscious leaders that the meaning of our communication is embedded in the response we get from others and that we should accept responsibility for our social results, then we can reflect on our social feedback and identify how we can change our strategies to generate different social results and interpretations on the part of followers. This situation calls for perceptual agility which involves building upon our powers of empathy and rapport. Relationship management through mastery of intra- and interpersonal skills is at the heart of conscious leadership practice.

For conscious leadership to emerge, this requires a willingness to shift from a fixed mindset to a growth mindset in relation to personal development. For example, one can imagine a situation where a coach meets with the potential leader who is not modelling presence and attentiveness and timeliness in relation to their interactions with their team members. The coach points this mismatch out to the potential leader and invites them to empathise with their staff. The potential leader may adopt a fixed mindset towards the opportunity for self-reflection and personal development in relation to this learning moment. Also, they could be adopting an emotionally charged defensive attitude. Either way, no personal development will occur. If, however, the potential leader is open to being open and really listening and frames the encounter with the coach as an opportunity for personal growth and to emerge as a more effective leader, then this would be fully enabled by and understood as adopting a healthy growth mindset. Either way, it is always a question of choice once the dynamics have been exposed at a conscious level of thought.

Conclusion

This is a book about conscious leadership. To understand conscious leadership, we must also have an appreciation of mindset, what it is, how it forms and how it shapes our personality and guides our decisions and social interactions.

Mindset, therefore, is the most important aspect of our lived experience in this world. Through our mindsets, we filter, make sense of and act on the social world, and so, our mindset has a significant impact upon the quality of both our lived experience and our social results. Our mindsets drive our emotional, cognitive and behavioural states, and so, whether we have a happy or sad experience, it is driven by our choice of mindset. We also know that it is often the case that most people, most of the time, are blissfully unaware of the state of their various mindsets, their historical antecedents, the beliefs and values that they are responsible for and the way in which they influence the way people choose to relate to us. This means that to be an effective leader, one must be reflective regarding the mindsets we adopt for a given situation and how resourceful they are in that moment, for ourselves and for our potential followers. This process of mindset reflection is called conscious leadership. In the next chapter, we will explore leadership in terms of defining the process, and we will differentiate conscious leadership from general leadership.

References

Dilts, R. (2018) *Changing Belief Systems with NLP*. Dilts Strategy Group.

Dweck, C.S. (2012) *Mindset: How You Can Fulfil Your Potential*. Constable & Robinson.

Grimley, B. (2019) *The 7Cs of Coaching: A Personal Journey Through the World of NLP and Coaching Psychology*. Routledge Taylor-Francis Group.

James, T. (2017) *Timeline Therapy and the Basis of Personality*. Crown House Publishing.

Keating, L. & Heslin, P. (2015) The Potential Role of Mindsets in Unleashing Employee Engagement. *Human Resource Management Review*, 25(10), p. 1016.

Maio, R.G., Haddock, G. & Verplanken, B. (2018) *The Psychology of Attitudes and Attitude Change*. Sage Publications Limited.

Nickerson, R. (1998) Confirmation Bias: A Ubiquitous Phenomenon in Many Guises. *Review of General Psychology*, 2, pp. 175–220. doi:10.1037/1089-2680.

O'Connor, J. & Seymour, J. (2011) *Introducing NLP: Psychological Skills for Understanding and Influencing People*. Conari Press

3   INTRODUCING LEADERSHIP

Introduction

Leadership is a hugely contested area within organisational science. The literature has an abundant range of leadership models and theories (Sveningsson and Larsson, 2006). This chapter concentrates on developing an understanding of leadership as a meta-model that stands above and, thus, influences all of its subordinate derivative leadership models. What is required is a clear definition of leadership as a meta-model that all other leadership models and theories are derivatives of. This chapter also explores what leadership is not as well as what it is.

Defining leadership

The literature on leadership is vast. It is beyond the scope of this chapter to compose a review as there are already extensive reviews (Grint, 2005; Northouse, 2010; Alvesson et al., 2017). Therefore, the emphasis of this section will be on offering a definition of leadership that appears to make sense in relation to the world of organisation and which can be understood in accessible and practical terms. As stated above, our aim is to identify a theory and definition of leadership that operates as a meta-model of leadership from which all other models are understood as derivatives. We borrow from the work of Smircich and Morgan (1982) and Alvesson et al. (2017), who consider leaders as people who influence the meanings that emerging followers attach to situations and who are successful at defining social situations and influencing the internal shaping of beliefs and values in relation to followers. Alvesson et al. (2017, p. 8) claim that: "Leaders are interpersonally trying to define meaning/reality for others who are inclined to (on a largely voluntary basis) accept such meaning-making and reality-defining acts". The empirical test regarding the existence of leadership is the existence of followers. Put simply, people follow a leader if that person defines social reality in ways that they are prepared to accept and act upon. In the absence of followers, one does not have leadership.

Alvesson et al. (2017) warn of the danger of interpreting employees' states of acquiescence as followership, meaning they take an internal decision to

DOI: 10.4324/9781003272793-4

hold back their point of view and "agree to agree" with their manager, imitating a state of followership when, in actual fact, it may be a state of subordination in the face of a senior figure with authority to define certain social situations and to instruct staff to act on these definitions. The evidence that someone is in a leadership role is the authentic voluntary acceptance of their efforts at influencing the meanings others attach to their experiences and to social situations and accepting their implicit or explicit directions regarding acting on that experience.

Leaders, therefore, are "meaning-makers" who offer potential followers socially constructed definitions of situations as, once people internalise and identify with them, they are moving into a followership role (Smircich and Morgan, 1982). Once the leader and follower have internalised shared beliefs and understandings, then the leader can, if required, suggest a course of action and lead the behaviours of followers. This view of leadership, thus, emphasises the socially constructed nature of leadership and the processual and relational dynamics that are central to the social construction process.

Smircich and Morgan (1982) claim that leadership involves a sense-making process. It involves framing and reframing of both the content and context that give situations significance, and it is from successful framing or reframing of situations that leaders derive the additional influence to lead and encourage the expression of specific behaviours, actions and emotions from followers in relation to a specific task. Essentially, leadership is a subjective process involving the social construction of reality to provide the foundations for collective action.

The social constructionist view of leaders as meaning-makers explains how people can be both managers and leaders. As managers, they are empowered by the organisation with the authority to define social situations in accordance with cultural norms. Staff, or subordinates, are expected to respect these definitions and act in accordance with the expectations of the manager. Whilst this is an influencing process, it is transactional and generally does not require any critical reflection on the part of the subordinate regarding the validity of the manager's definitions or their implied or explicit requests for action. All that is required is passive acceptance and attending to the wishes of the manager. This transactional process may involve influence due to the subordinate agreeing to be influenced in return for a salary though this is not conscious leadership as we define conscious leadership. In contrast, this is crude transactional leadership.

If the manager offers a definition, a framing of a situation or a reframe that subordinates are prepared to internalise and accept as valid and act upon, then we can define this as a leadership/followership dynamic. Thus, leadership requires followers to give up their own rights to socially construct a situation and subordinate these in favour of the leader's framing and reframing activities. Such social dynamics at the group and intergroup levels explain why securing a broad leadership base is so challenging and why conflict often emerges over contested meanings and frames and reframes of social reality between different factions and competing potential leaders throughout the organisation. Smircich and Morgan (1982) provide a theoretical framework for understanding the leadership process:

1. Leadership is best understood as essentially a social process enabled through social constructions and interaction.
2. Leadership involves a process of framing and reframing social reality in ways that are deemed acceptable and valid to followers.
3. Leadership is an asymmetrical relationship which is unequal as the follower surrenders their own subjective frames of reference to define and interpret reality in favour of the leader's. This is an act of power.

Clearly, leadership involves an intensely socially interactive and intersubjective process of sense-making, rapport-building and dialogue. Leadership must also involve a matching process at the level of beliefs, values, attitudes, emotional expressions, behaviours and thinking styles. We know that when someone attempts to offer leadership, if they are deemed too far removed from the established culture of the group whom they are trying to lead, there is a significant probability that they will be rejected. This is the paradox of leadership that suggests that to lead a problem like cultural change, we must, as potential leaders, closely match with the established cultural norms we are trying to reframe as dysfunctional.

Reflective leadership

This process we call leadership can be enhanced if we adopt a reflective approach to it that involves raising our levels of conscious awareness regarding the way we draw upon internal resources such as our beliefs, values, attitudes, ideas, emotions and thinking styles and our external resources such as our behaviours and interactive strategies. Thus, we are making a distinction between intra- and interpersonal skills development. Intra-reflexivity involves reflection upon the utility and resourcefulness of our internal resources, and inter-reflexivity involves a similar process of reflexivity regarding our behaviours and related social interactions. For the purpose of this book, we define the use of our intra- and interpersonal skills as our strategies.

Reflexivity, which Alvesson et al. (2017, p. 14) define as: "The ambition to carefully and systematically take a critical view of one's own assumptions, ideas and favoured vocabulary and to consider if alternative ones make sense", is a key leadership competence in the model that we are developing. Reflexivity is closely related to "reflection", which Alvesson et al. (2017, p. 13) define as: "An important human activity in which people recapture their experience, think about it, mull it over and evaluate it". Reflection, therefore, is another core competency that potential leaders could master to improve their chances of establishing themselves as leaders with voluntary followers. The absence of reflexive and reflective leadership efforts, either consciously or intuitively, may explain the failure of attempts at leadership.

Leadership as a soft skill

There is a general understanding throughout the academic and practitioner communities that a fundamental problem that plagues change management projects is the lack of awareness amongst managers regarding the critical importance of soft skills. The trend seems to be that managers value developing their hard cognitive, analytical and planning skills over their soft intra and interpersonal skills. The former involves our ability to self-regulate our emotions, thinking and behavioural patterns and the latter fundamentally involves our social skills for managing productive relationships. This situation is starting to change with many organisations accessing the field of coaching which aims to improve the soft change management skills of management practitioners. In many ways it is this need for the development of soft skills that has motivated the writing of this book. It is critical that managers as leaders learn to balance their commitment to developing both their soft and hard skills. The need for leaders to be open to building their soft skills requires them to feel psychologically safe to do so. They often are reluctant to be introspective and open to such change as they feel uncomfortable doing so. The reasons that leadership fails to emerge in many situations include variables such as:

- Weak rapport building.
- Poor standards of communication.
- Tendency towards a fixed mindset.
- Lack of stakeholder engagement.
- Absence of psychological safety in groups.
- Lack of team integration.

These fault lines all have at least one thing in common, which is that they indicate a general weakness regarding intra- and interpersonal skills within many management teams whose members are expected not only to manage but also to provide leadership when it is required. This means that we need a model of leadership which focuses on the micro aspects of what actually happens when a person establishes a leadership role with a group that self-identify as followers who voluntarily accept the proposed definitions, i.e., the framing or reframing schemes, presented by their leader for internal consumption and organised future action. This process of focus we refer to as reflexivity and reflection and locate these two activities under the heading of "conscious leadership".

Leadership is a scarce commodity

According to popular wisdom, leadership is not that uncommon. Alvesson et al. (2017) take a very critical view of leadership and especially the common wisdom around leadership in their book *Leadership Reflexivity*. They claim that, far from being a fundamental aspect of the organisation of work, leadership is actually not that common. Alvesson et al. (2017) also argue that some organisations may not require leadership as a means for organising work. For example, in knowledge-intensive organisations such as university settings, academics who mainly work in autonomous groups or even alone for extended periods may not require leadership.

In every organisation throughout the world, we are led to believe that we should find managers generating leadership through creating followers to lead their organisations through transformational change. This is an example of smoking mirrors, a framing exercise which advances the premise that organisations are being led, which, in reality, when one looks at the empirical evidence, is incredibly misleading regarding what is actually going on in organisations; in many cases, it is not leadership (Alvesson et al., 2017).

Many managers, particularly senior managers, are "expected" to generate leadership and convert subordinates into followers. In order to meet these expectations, many managers simply internalise a self-narrative that promotes the delusion that they are, in fact, leaders, that they do have followers and that they are providing important leadership. However, when one looks hard for the evidence, the concrete nature of these delusions becomes very clear.

Thus, to understand leadership in action, one needs to analyse the interactive processes underpinning drivers of influence between high influential people and low influential people that allegedly generate leadership effects; this requires in-depth longitudinal micro qualitative studies of organisational case studies (Sveningsson and Larsson, 2006) which are expensive and time-consuming to achieve and, thus, are not common. Leadership, in sum, is considered by Alvesson et al. (2017) as a mode of organising, and one that is required to organise unique organisational challenges. An interesting framework for thinking about leadership as a mode for problem-solving was developed by Grint (2005), who introduces the idea of wicked, critical and tame problems, which are helpful to understanding when leadership, or perhaps management, would be required.

A tame problem

A tame problem is a problem defined by Grint (2008, p, 12) as: "A Tame Problem may be complicated, but it is resolvable through uni-linear acts and it is likely to have occurred before." Consequently, for tame problems, leadership is not required, management is. Managers can rely upon their previous experience to the perceived problem to establish the correct solution and it will naturally follow that it will be solved. This point is one that can be very challenging to managers self-conception as leaders of their teams.

A critical problem

A critical problem is defined by Grint (2008, p. 13) as: "A crisis presented as self-evident in nature as encapsulating very little time for decision making and action and is often associated with authoritarianism." Within organisations senior managers may construct a view of a problem as critical so that they may legitimise immediate action rather than engage in critical thinking thus claiming their right to manage as experts. A significant problem with this approach is that often the problem is wrongly constructed. The symptom is treated as the problem and, thus, the real substantive problem remains unchallenged. This is not leadership; it is another form of management using vertical power relationships to mobilise consent. Critical problems are very common throughout organisations as they support the view of management competency and power to act and to instruct others how to act. They also reduce anxiety and provide a degree of assumed certainty that the critical problem can be resolved. These kinds of secondary gains are highly valued by transactional leaders and are a barrier to encouraging the possible reframing of the critical problem to one that is understood to be a wicked problem.

A wicked problem

Wicked problems are, essentially, novel and, where there are no previous solutions within the history of the organisation, available to be readily applied by members. For example, a need to change aspects of the culture of the organisation. In such a situation with this kind of wicked problem, leadership is required. Grint (2008, p. 13) claims that: "The leader's role with a Wicked Problem, therefore, is to ask the right questions rather than provide the right answers because the answers may not be self-evident and will require a collaborative process to make any kind of progress".

Therefore, wicked problems are not solved using dramatic interventions based on transactional and command and control authority. Wicked problems require leadership supported by management. They require a more sophisticated and thoughtful approach, a reflexive approach demanding highly honed intra- and interpersonal skills to generate a field of collaboration through which stakeholders can express themselves. This is the aim of conscious leadership.

It is important that, when researching leadership, we differentiate between alternative modes of organising, leadership and pseudo leadership, i.e., the world of make-believe. We need a clear definition of leadership that can be empirically evaluated and tested against set criteria and which can form the basis of leadership development projects that are rooted in valid definitions and which do not become fantasy projects.

On leadership/followership becoming

In our understanding of leadership, the generation and retention of followers is a key characteristic (Alvesson et al., 2017). In the absence of voluntary followers, for us, there is no leadership. Managers may attempt to build a leadership identity though they must also try to encourage others to adopt a followership identity. The question is, how do followers emerge? Are they created by emerging leaders? Do emerging leaders have special qualities or traits that stimulate the generation of followers in a causal and mechanical way? In cultural studies, it is conventionally understood, based on qualitative research, that followers accept leadership identities from people who share their cultural backgrounds (Hofstede et al., 2010). This indicates that followers project a leadership identity onto another person in the act of internalising the self-identity of a follower. However, this process is not asymmetrical; it is symmetrical because the leader must accept the follower to be the leader. So, we have, in effect, an exchange of identities. Thus, the crafting of a leadership identity involves the mutual crafting of a follower's identity, and so the process is essentially a socially interactive process. This raises interesting questions concerning power. The leader is dependent upon their followers for their leadership identity and the followers on the leader for their desired rewards.

An emerging leader who is in the process of what we could call "leadership/followership becoming" must build and sustain rapport with emerging followers. Emerging leaders must ensure that, at the levels of beliefs, values and related cultural norms, they match with their emerging followers. If they mismatch too early in the leadership becoming process, they will break rapport, and the mutual identity construction process between followers and leaders will stop. This means that emerging leaders must be reflexive; they must be reflexive towards their intra- and interpersonal skills if they are to manage the identity construction process intelligently and with awareness and then, if successful in their leadership applications, maintain productive leadership/followership relationships. This process of intra- and inter-reflexive relationship management is what conscious leadership is essentially concerned with.

Differentiating leadership from other modes of organising

Alvesson et al. (2017) generate a useful model that they call their 6M Framework (6 Modes of Organising) to differentiate between what leadership is and what it is not regarding models of organising the affairs of an enterprise (see Figure 3.1).

Starting with Leadership, the authors emphasise vertical persuasion based upon influencing through interpersonal relationships focusing on meaning-making and value systems. Then they identify management as top-down influencing, drawing from legitimate authority to define situations and organise resources. This is followed by "exercise of power", which basically relies on legitimate positional power to influence others. Next is the use of "networking and peer influence" based upon the exercise of collaboration and mutual advice-giving and taking. Then "team/group work" is highlighted as a source of peer group norms and pressure to conform to such norms. Finally, the authors cite the impact of "autonomous working" as a means of self-validation

Figure 3.1 Reflexive Leadership
Source: Alvesson et al. (2017)

in regards to one's standards at work and individual control over how one accomplishes the work.

It follows that there are at least six modes of organising and influencing work-based processes. All six modes of organising do involve the application of influencing tools although only leadership is relevant at this stage. Many managers who claim to be practising leadership may, in fact, be using any one or more of the alternative modes of organisation as described by Alvesson et al. in their 6M model.

Alvesson et al. (2017) identify leadership as just one way in which organisations can organise their affairs. They differentiate leadership from organising through autonomous teams, management, teamwork, the use of coercive power and through networks of peer groups by the emphasis on targeting meanings and values to provide motivational inspiration and moral support as legitimate role models. Management, in contrast, relies upon legitimate control.

The leadership drivers that produce followership, the authors claim, are dialogue, reflexivity and mutual feedback. Rather than being a significant presence in organisations, they claim it is, in actuality, quite rare. Their 6M model is useful when it comes to differentiating between leadership as a mode of organisation and any other one of the five remaining modes.

Conclusion

Leaders are required to frame reality in ways that generate collective enquiry and action on the part of followers. They must live in the present and in the future. They must build a culture that attends to day-to-day operations as well as attending to the organisational development activities that generate organisational fitness for the future. They must build a culture which maximises the development of people and productivity (Blake and Mouton, 1964). They must balance their focus on ambition with their focus on community service (Dilts, 2017). It is no longer good enough for leaders to emphasise financial profit as the main profit construct. Bringing more of something into the world that benefits society at large as well as financial profit is an important profit criterion (Kobjoll, 2000). How staff are managed matters. The style of managers, and leaders, matters. The beliefs and values they adhere to matter. The strategies used to define and generate profit matter. Uniting and engaging stakeholders behind a shared vision and ambition matters. Ultimately building an engaged stakeholder network matters.

Thus, leadership is tough and demanding and requires emotional resilience (Dilts, 2017). Leadership involves building an organisation that is fit for the future through collaborative work practices (Dilts, 2016). Alvesson et al. (2017) acknowledge that leadership requires reflexivity on the part of the highly influential person if they are to both establish and maintain leadership/followership relationships. Leaders, thus, need highly developed emotional intelligence as well as cognitive intelligence (Goleman, 1995). These qualities we have highlighted regarding what needs to be true for someone to be demonstrating leadership effects require a conscious leadership mindset.

Finally, to understand how leadership/followership emerges as a socially constructed process of identity becoming, we need to integrate our leadership perspectives. In the next chapter, we will present and explore our model of integrated leadership theory through which we initially review the model of transactional and transformational of Bass and Avolio (1990) to highlight key elements of the leadership/followership becoming process.

References

Alvesson, M., Blom, M. & Sveningsson, S. (2017) *Reflexive Leadership: Organising in an Imperfect World*. Sage.

Bass, B.M. & Avolio, B.J. (1990) The Implications of Transactional and Transformational Leadership for Individual, Team, and Organizational Development. *Research in Organizational Change and Development*, 4, pp. 231–272.

Blake, R. & Mouton, J. (1964) *The Managerial Grid: Key Orientations for Achieving Production Through People*. Gulf Publications.

Dilts, R. (2016) *Generative Collaboration*. Dilts Strategy Group.

Dilts, R. (2017) *Conscious Leadership and Resilience*. Dilts Strategy Group.

Goleman, D. (1995) *Emotional Intelligence*. Bantam Books, Inc.

Grint, K. (2005) Problems, Problems, Problems: The Social Construction of Leadership. *Human Relations*, 58(11), pp. 1467–1494.

Grint, K. (2008) Wicked Problems and Clumsy Solutions: The Role of Leadership. *Clinical Leader*, 1(11).

Hofstede, G., Hofstede, G.J. & Minkov, M. (2010) *Cultures and Organizations: Software of the Mind*, 3rd edn. McGraw-Hill Professional.

Kobjoll, K. (2000) *Adventure European Quality Award*. Orell Fussli Verlag.

Northouse, P. (2010) *Leadership Theory and Practice*. Sage.

Smircich, L. & Morgan, G. (1982) Leadership: The Management of Meaning. *Journal of Applied Behavioural Science*, 18, pp. 257–273.

Sveningsson, S. & Larsson, M. (2006) Fantasies of Leadership: Identity Work. *Leadership*, 2, pp. 203–224.

4 TRANSACTIONAL AND TRANSFORMATIONAL LEADERSHIP

Introduction

This chapter explores a model of leadership that integrates key elements of transactional and transformational leadership theory to unpack the critical success factors that contribute to successful leadership/followership becoming. We initially take a critical look at the assumption that transactional leadership differs from alternative leadership models because it is based upon an exchange between leaders and followers. We focus upon the belief that transactional leadership places emphasis upon extrinsic rewards as a source of influence. Then we examine transformational leadership and identify similarities with transactional leadership and key differences. The key source of influence attracting followers for transformational leadership, we argue, is intrinsic rewards (Herzberg et al., 1959). We review each of the four key elements of transformational leadership which influence the framing of intrinsic rewards that attract followers, which Bass (1985) identifies as the Four Is or the Four Elements of transformational leadership.

The additive effect model of leadership explored

Bass and Avolio (1990) have generated a very useful model of leadership which integrates two separate theories of leadership (see Figure 4.1): transactional and transformational leadership, which they call the "Additive Effect".

The underlying theory is that the two leadership styles can be understood to be in a linear relationship. Bass and Avolio (1990) argue that it is the additive effect of the discrete elements of the two leadership (transactional and transformational) models that give rise to higher-level leadership outcomes of a transformational nature. The additive effect leadership model is useful to practitioners because of its conceptual elegance and parsimonious explanation of what is actually an incredibly complex social and cultural phenomenon. Both transactional and transformational leadership models are a derivative of leadership as the meta-model discussed in Chapter 3. They both target beliefs and values, although they are mediated through different forms of motivation (Herzberg, 1987).

DOI: 10.4324/9781003272793-5

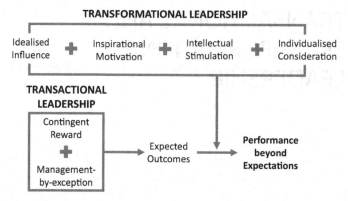

Figure 4.1 The Additive Effect of Transformational Leadership

Source: Adapted from Bass and Avolio (1990)

Transactional leadership

Transactional leadership has been defined as a relationship between a leader and a follower that occurs: "When a leader exchanges something of economic, political, or psychological value with a follower". (Whittington et al., 2009, p. 1861). This is a very functional form of leadership that mainly operates at the level of extrinsic motivation, which involves rewards that are instrumental in nature, such as money, status, recognition, lieu time, promotion, company perks, political and, at times, psychological support (Herzberg, 1987). Transactional leadership is arguably the dominant leadership style operating throughout the western world. Transactional leadership underpins the principles of scientific management (Taylor, 1911), which are based on a model of rational economic man. The basic principle that underpins transactional leadership is that the leader offers an implicit or explicit reward to the follower in return for their co-operation and application to achieve a specific task. This reward, if valued by the follower, creates the basis of influence that binds the transactional leader and their follower together. Once the task is complete and the reward given, the leadership dynamic vanishes. So, the first principle is that transactional leadership is dependent upon a "contingent reward" that is valued by potential followers and within the power of the leader to grant to the follower.

The principle of contingent reward generates the second principle of transactional leadership, which is that transactional leadership, in general, will not generate outstanding outcomes in performance on the part of followers; rather, it will generate "expected outcomes" which are defined as basic standards of performance which broadly meet with stakeholder expectations. Transactional leadership can be a very effective form of organising. When followers are in a relationship with a transactional leader, they can often enjoy feelings of stability, productive working relationships with the transactional leader, and feel psychologically safe. These outcomes derive from having very clear performance expectations and explicit methods for managing tasks that are often laid down within Standard Operating Procedures and cultural norms, emphasising respect and harmony between leaders and followers. When involved in a state of rapport with their transactional leaders, followers will often feel competent and confident that they can achieve what is expected of them (Campbell et al., 2003). The transactional leader may also offer a paternalistic dynamic and enjoy guiding and, when necessary, explaining how best to approach a specific task. This means that when transactional leaders also utilise a "situational approach" (Hersey and Blanchard, 1969) to their leadership approach, the probability of the effectiveness of the transactional approach can be increased. The situational approach basically involves the transactional leader assessing each task to be allocated in relation to the experience of followers and their competency with regards to successfully managing the task and delivering upon expected outcomes. Hersey and Blanchard (1969) established four influencing strategies for enabling the leader/follower relationship they labelled "Directing", "Coaching", "Supporting" and finally, "Delegating".

Their model provides the transactional leader with a set of four clear social strategies which the authors refer to as "leadership styles", though they can also be interpreted as social strategies for enabling productive working relationships which are inherently functional and which aim to achieve a work task to an expected outcome. This means that adopting a transactional leadership style is not necessarily an impoverished leadership strategy; it can be, and often is, a very appropriate, effective and versatile leadership strategy assuming that the individual is open to such behavioural flexibility and leadership development. What the model lacks is an explanation of how one learns to adopt any one of the four leadership styles and the role of reflexivity and personal development as catalysts for such deep structure learning to occur. However, the transactional leadership style can also be a very ineffective form of organising. Three themes that can help analyse potential flaws with transactional leadership are: (1) management by exception passive; (2) management by exception active; and (3) personal style of the transactional leader.

Management by exception passive

This form of management involves very low personal identification on the part of the transactional leader and follower. The relationship is purely functional, and the follower is often perceived as a tool or a resource to enable task achievement as directed by the manager. This style of management behaviour is associated with interventions of a corrective nature being made on the part of the transactional leader into the performance of a follower only when a problem regarding performance is brought to the manager's attention and only when the problem has manifested to an extent that it can no longer be ignored. This behavioural strategy, often referred to as passive leadership, can, in some cases, create a disassociated state in the follower and dilute positive staff engagement with the task, the leader and the organisation at large (Crystal and Holtz, 2014). The follower will feel that their "leader" is not interested in either themselves as a human being or the actual work and is only interested in "ticking boxes", so they may produce expected outcomes that are significantly below the standard that they are actually capable of doing.

Management by exception active

This form of management can also involve very low personal identification on the part of the transactional leader and their follower. The behavioural strategy adopted involves the transactional leader actively monitoring the work of the employees and taking immediate corrective action. The transactional leader may be stuck in an ethnocentric view of the world and adopt a fixed mindset that is not open to stretching to a differentiated or integrated perspective with followers (Dixon, 1998). The main characteristic involves actively looking for problems or flaws in the performance of the employee. A lack of coaching, nurturing, clear direction and productive relationships are not uncommon. Both behavioural strategies (management by exception active or passive) lack the flexibility of the situational approach. Arguably, due to the personal style of the transactional leader, these leadership strategies may be fundamental to the understanding of disengagement levels that are cited as plaguing many western organisations.

Personal style of the transactional leader

Regardless of whether the transactional leader adopts management by exception active or passive, "how" they interact with followers has a significant impact upon leadership/follower relationships. Mencl et al. (2016, p. 636) argue that: *Effective leadership extends beyond traditional managerial authority, relying on influence through personal interactions and positive relationships*". Transactional leaders base their transactional approach on two dimensions: (1) constructive transactions; and (2) corrective transactions (Avolio, 1999). The first involves the clear explanation of expectations and the setting of objective criteria for achieving a reward in relation to task achievement. The second involves the transactional leader focusing more upon creating a change in the behaviour, standard of co-operation and/or the attitude of a potential follower. The former can be the basis for productive relationships, which can also be characterised by the COACH state, whilst the latter can be the basis for a lack of trust between follower and leader and the CRASH state. However, these effects are amplified by the personal behavioural style of the transactional leader, which either creates or breaks rapport between the leader and their followers.

Transactional leadership can generate productive follower/leadership dynamics if the transactional leader also purposefully adopts a conscious leadership mindset to build and sustain rapport with followers and establish a climate of mutual trust and respect. However, transactional leadership is appropriate for day-to-day, recurring tasks and for change projects of the first order variety; that is, change projects that involve extending established practices or modifying these, i.e., tame problems. When it comes to change of the second order (Levy and Merry, 1986), i.e., transformational change, perhaps involving a transformation in management mindset from a fixed to a growth model and the established culture that maintains the current status quo, we need a form of leadership that encourages extraordinary performance which transcends basic expected outcomes and generates performance beyond expectations; this is transformational leadership.

Transformational leadership

Transformational leadership has been defined as: "The leader moving the follower beyond immediate self-interests through idealized influence (charisma), inspiration, intellectual stimulation, or individualized consideration. It elevates the follower's level of maturity and ideals as well as concerns for achievement, self-actualization, and the well-being of others, the organization, and society". (Erkutlu, 2008, p. 709). We know from research that leadership representing the characteristics of the transformational model does generate higher levels of positive identification with the leader (Lowe et al., 1996) and the organisation (Testa, 2001) and increased job satisfaction (Bass and Avolio, 1994). Transformational leadership, according to Bass and Avoli (1990), relies upon four variables known as the Four Is: idealised influence (II); inspirational motivation (IM); intellectual stimulation (IS); and individualised consideration (IC). An additive effect can be understood as: "An effect in which two or more variables, used in combination in a model, produce a total effect that is the same as the sum of the individual effects" (Alatawi, 2017, p. 19).

Regarding idealised influence, the theory is that if a leader can be accepted as a role model on the part of followers, they will have influence over their followers because, as role models, they signify an "ideal" identity through their talents and/or values and beliefs (Mead, 1934; Blumer, 1969) that followers find truly inspirational. For example, an aspiring sportsperson may admire leaders in their field; for example, a tennis player learning their sport may have Andy Murray or Serena Williams as their role model, their ideal tennis player. This role model can also become a source of inspirational motivation for their followers. Inspirational motivation can be enhanced if the leader has a back story through which they overcame adversity to emerge as a champion or highly successful in their field, their own "heroes journey" from adversity to success, overcoming severe obstacles on their journey (Campbell, 1991).

The role model may be someone who stimulates followers intellectually. They may motivate followers to think deeply about a subject. For example, Steve Jobs was known for inspiring deep creative and conceptual thinking throughout his team when in charge of Apple. Paulo Reglus Neves Freire, the Brazilian educator and philosopher, inspired hundreds of thousands of followers to use education to emancipate poor and/or economically oppressed communities throughout the world. The American Professor of Anthropology, Ruth Benedict, inspired a movement of women entering academic professions.

Finally, the role model may be someone who also generates a belief in followers that they care about their welfare and personal development and so establish influence through individual consideration. Examples of high-profile transformational leaders are readily available in literature. For examples, Dr Martin Luther King and his Civil Rights movement, Nelson Mandela and breaking up Apartheid, Mother Teresa and services to the poor, and Margaret Thatcher who transformed the economic state of the United Kingdom through market restructuring and public sector reforms, are four high profile examples of building transformational leadership dynamics through the interplay of the Four Is as sources of motivation for followers to achieve extraordinary social change.

The "additive effect" is possibly rare in terms of all four factors influencing each other equally to generate followers. Research has suggested, strongly, that one of these factors in isolation, if acknowledged in the leader by a critical mass of followers, can motivate a mass of support in an organisation or a community behind a transformational change process (Alatawi, 2017). Therefore, we do not argue that all four factors need to be identified by followers in order to generate transformational leadership outcomes, though it does make intuitive sense that if followers do identify all Four Is in their choice of leader, then the source of leadership/followership relations, and thus influence, will be so much stronger and more resilient.

Transformational leadership is also exemplified in organisational settings when an individual motivates a wider group of followers to achieve the highest levels of performance to transform an aspect of the overarching organisational system. For example, economic, technological, product, market position or cultural transformation. Sometimes the change focus is on all five change targets, or it may be specific to individual elements. The aim is to literally transform the established state into something that is completely different in form.

On the question of motivation

Central to leadership dynamics is the mediating effect of motivation. Whilst all leadership models require a transaction to enable influence over followers on the part of leaders, the nature of these transactions can be understood productively as either belonging to categories of intrinsic or extrinsic motivation (Herzberg et al., 1959). In order to understand how leadership works in practice, we need to understand how motivation works as an enabler of leadership influence over followers on the part of leaders. Followers need to have their motivations satisfied regardless of the nature of the leadership dynamic (transactional or transformational). They need financial reward and security of employment. Transactional leaders who are also paternalistic and benevolent can also satisfy the third need in Maslow's (1954) hierarchy, the need to feel that you belong to a group and have a skill that is of value to the group. In the transaction, this need can be validated, especially if the style of the transactional leader is respectful and personable in relation to the follower.

The first three basic foundational needs of Maslow's model:

1. Physiological.
2. Safety.
3. Belongingness.

could be interpreted as "Hygiene Factors" (Herzberg et al. 1959); that is to say that their presence is not a sustainable motivator that is consciously significant to the follower, though their absence can have immediate psychological effects leading to acute anxiety and CRASH state. When our employment is secure, we tend not to think about it; we are neither motivated nor demotivated. However, when we are threatened with redundancy, this triggers acute anxiety as our need for stability, safety and connection is being destabilised. This lack of motivational drive also explains why transactional leaders, even when they have built quality relations with followers based upon rapport, may inspire average performance and achieve expected outcomes as the higher motivational needs such as esteem and self-actualisation are not being tapped into and the basic lower needs, once satisfied, go relatively unnoticed. Building on Maslow's model, Herzberg et al. (1959) call for an understanding and appreciation of what they call "motivational factors", which basically involve satisfying self and group esteem needs and offering opportunities for growth and development to followers so that they may access self-actualisation opportunities. When attempting transformational change, all levels of motivation in Maslow's model need to be cultivated and made accessible to followers, and thus, both hygiene and motivational drivers are being used resourcefully to establish a culture of transformational leadership and change enabled through conscious awareness.

More recently, in his insightful book *Drive*, author Daniel Pink (2018) presents his revised conceptualisation of motivational theory which builds on the work of motivational theorists such as Maslow (1954) and Herzberg et al. (1959). Pink advocates for a three-tiered model of motivation based upon the metaphor of "operating systems" similar to a computer programme that leaders tap into to influence followers; these are:

Motivation 1: This is the very first level of Maslow's hierarchy of needs which is the primaeval requirement for resources to provide shelter, clothing, heat, water and food. This is a fundamental motivational resource that is culturally wired into all human beings. We saw this motivational driver being very publicly activated during the 2020 COVID-19 crisis when supermarket shelves were cleared and left empty and people started hoarding provisions. However, this source of motivation is a hygiene factor and is only dramatically active when we fear that we will no longer be able to access the resources we need to basically survive. The threat of redundancy or dismissal does act as a control mechanism; however, it is a short term influencing strategy that creates a CRASH state and negative identification on the part of potential followers, and this is not a healthy resourceful social dynamic for organisations embedded in an ever increasingly competitive and changing world.

Motivation 2: This is the cultural system of reward and punishment which dominates many countries throughout the world. If you do well, you get a reward, and if you fail, you get punished. Classic carrot and stick conditioning strategy. The problem with this influencing strategy, Pink (2018) argues, is that it is short term in terms of motivational drive. Further, it can generate a narrow task perspective on the part of followers which seeks only to achieve the task, often at the expense of other variables. For example, a transactional leader may introduce a bonus system for producing higher levels of profit in a hospitality business such as a hotel and, as a result, staff costs get cut back, materials are sourced that are the most economically advantageous, training gets removed as a cost and, as a result, profit increases in the short term though at the cost of staff morale, customer satisfaction, product and service quality and market competitiveness. The lack of strategic, long-term thinking and visioning is also a significant symptom of motivation model 2 in operation.

Motivation 3: This operating system of motivational drivers is based upon the theory of self-fulfilment and psychological needs, such as a need to feel connected with a group and their leader. A belief that we are accepted and valued and that our leaders truly "see" and "hear" us (Bubler, 1923). A feeling that what we are doing is worthwhile and is making a difference in the world at a level of impact. Gaining opportunities to grow and develop our potential as human beings. Being intellectually stimulated and having a role model whom we can trust and respect and who provides us with a source of validation of our worth to the group. Sensing that our ambitions, mission, vision and purpose are fully integrated and at one with the organisation. This model of motivation is concerned with accessing intrinsic motivational drivers.

Conscious leadership and Motivation 3

Daniel Pink's (2018) theory of Motivation 3 is the theory of motivation that is most closely related to the principles of conscious leadership. It involves, in practice, the leader consciously trying to be fully present when interacting with followers and making a concerted effort to relate to them personally and respect their view of the world (Bowman and Bowman, 2014). It also involves paying attention to what they say and the beliefs and values that generate their perspectives. Seeing and confirming the positive intentions behind followers' attitudes and actions from a place of respect and curiosity, and not judgement, is important (Bowman and Bowman, 2014). Confirming the potential of followers to grow and develop and actively seeking out opportunities to enable this self-actualisation process is an act of conscious leadership. Making an effort to build and sustain rapport with followers and relate to them in their terms and establishing trust involves conscious leadership practices (Campbell et al., 2003).

Conclusion

In this chapter, our aim was to demonstrate that transformational leadership is dependent on transactional motivations between both followers and leaders, involving intrinsic reward systems. Acting with conscious awareness, leaders establish a sense of COACH state in their followers who, in return, positively identify with the transformational leader, their perspectives and their aims. Crucially, transformational leadership does require a conscious leadership mindset and a firm foundation of transactional leadership characterised by productive working relationships between followers and leaders based on rapport and a climate of mutual trust for its manifestation. We recognise the need for a situationally contingent model for enacting transactional and/or transformational leadership. For example, within a building site constructing houses, perhaps a day-to-day culture of high-quality transactional leadership would be the appropriate leadership model, and, in contrast, in the NHS, transformational leadership supported by a form of transactional leadership would be appropriate, assuming the pressing need to completely redesign the service was awakened in enough stakeholders' mindsets.

Transformational leadership involves second order change, whilst transactional in isolation involves first order change or day-to-day operations. Conscious leadership not only supports the manifestation of authentic transformational leadership, but it also may support and address deficiencies in transactional leadership caused by crude management by exception (active or passive) and active dissociation between manager and staff and overt reliance on task orientation. This means that the key developmental issue is one of "personal style": do you manage through a transactional style wrapped in a conscious leadership mindset or an anti-conscious leadership mindset? Finally, transformational leadership can be activated by one or more of the Four Is being recognised on the part of followers as integral aspects of the identity of their leader of choice. It may be the exception to the norm that transformational leaders are acknowledged as possessing all four of the Is as core personal qualities on the part of followers. In the following chapter, we introduce the idea of the leadership paradox to explain the basic mistake that many organisations make by oversimplifying the process involved in embedding the additive effect into its leadership culture.

References

Alatawi, A.W. (2017) The Myth of the Additive Effect of the Transformational Leadership Model. *Contemporary Management Research*, 13(1), pp. 19–30.

Avolio, B. (1999) *Full Leadership Development: Building the Vital Forces in Organizations*. Sage Publications.

Bass, B.M. (1985) *Leadership and Performance Beyond Expectation*. Free Press.

Bass, B.M. & Avolio, B.J. (1990) The Implications of Transactional and Transformational Leadership for Individual, Team, and Organizational Development. *Research in Organizational Change and Development*, 4, pp. 231–272.

Bass, B.M. & Avolio, B.J. (Eds.). (1994) *Improving Organizational Effectiveness Through Transformational Leadership*. Sage Publications, Inc.

Blumer, H. (1969) *Symbolic Interactionism*. University of California Press.

Bowman, S. & Bowman, C. (2014) *Conscious Leadership: The Key to Unlocking Success*. Access Consciousness Publishing Company.

Bubler, M. (1923) *Ich und Du*. Im Insel-Verlag zu Leipzig.

Campbell, J. (1991) *The Hero's Journey*. New World Library.

Campbell, K., White, C. & Johnson, D. (2003) Leader-Member Relations as a Function of Rapport Management. *Journal of Business Communication*, 40, pp. 170–194.

Crystal, H. & Holtz, B. (2014) The Effects of Passive Leadership on Workplace Incivility. *Journal of Organizational Behavior*, 35(4).

Dixon, N.M. (1998) *Dialogue at Work*. Lemos & Crane.

Erkutlu, H. (2008) The Impact of Transformational Leadership on Organizational and Leadership Effectiveness: The Turkish Case. *Journal of Management Development*, 27(7), pp. 708–726.

Hersey, P. & Blanchard, K.H. (1969) Life Cycle Theory of Leadership. *Training and Development Journal*, 23(5), pp. 26–34.

Herzberg, F. (1987) One More Time: How Do You Motivate Employees? *Harvard Business Review*, 81(1), pp. 87–96.

Herzberg, F., Mausner, B. & Snyderman, B.B. (1959) *The Motivation to Work*. Transaction Publishers.

Levy, A. & Merry, U. (1986) *Organizational Transformation: Approaches, Strategies, Theories*. Praeger.

Lowe, K.B., Kroeck, K.G. & Sivasubramaniam, N. (1996) Effectiveness Correlates of Transformational and Transactional Leadership: A Meta-Analytic Review of the MLQ Literature. *The Leadership Quarterly*, 7, pp. 385–415.

Maslow, H.A. (1954) *Motivation and Personality*, 3rd edn. Addison Wesley.

Mead, H.G. (1934) *Mind, Self and Society, from the Stand Point of a Social Behaviourist*. University of Chicago Press.

Mencl, J., Wefald, A. & Ittersum, K. (2016) Transformational Leader Attributes: Interpersonal Skills, Engagement, and Well-Being. *Leadership & Organization Development Journal*, 37, pp. 635–657.

Pink, D. (2018) *Drive: The Surprising Truth About What Motivates Us*. Cannon Gate.

Taylor, F.W. (1911) The *Principles of Scientific Management*. W.W. Norton and Company.

Testa, M. (2001) Organizational Commitment, Job Satisfaction, and Effort in the Service Environment. *The Journal of Psychology*, 135, pp. 226–236.

Whittington, J.L., Coker, R.H., Goodwin, V.L., Ickes, W. & Murray, B. (2009) Transactional Leadership Revisited: Self-Other Agreement and Its Consequences. *Journal of Applied Social Psychology*, 39, pp. 1860–1886. doi:10.1111/j.1559-1816.

5   THE LEADERSHIP PARADOX

Introduction

The Additive Effect Model has been, and remains, a very useful tool for explaining, conceptually, a series of important variables that impact the leadership/follower dynamic. However, its significant weakness is that, in many ways, it remains largely conceptual and perhaps lacks clear and explicit practical powers of application. It can often beguile managers into "falsely" believing that the model seems straightforward and easy to understand; therefore, in practice, it must be relatively unproblematic with regard to actualisation. However, in practice, mastering the model and the capabilities required to enact daily behaviours and outcomes associated with each of the Four Is is very difficult and requires personal commitment towards continuous learning and personal improvement. Also, there is a tendency for potential leaders to positively, both socially and intellectually, identify with the additive effect as a leadership model whilst behaving consistently in ways that run counter to the model. We usefully refer to this phenomenon as "the leadership paradox".

Leadership behaviours "in action" may often combine contradictory features or qualities when compared to the potential leader's espoused theory of their ideal leadership identity. These ideas have been theoretically developed and advanced through action-orientated research into both inhibitors and enablers of organisational learning by Argyris and Schön (1996). This chapter revisits the theory of Argyris and Schön and explains how their theory and conceptual framework of double loop learning in organisations can shine a torch on both conscious leadership and in extreme cases, anti-conscious leadership practices. Specifically, this chapter will explore in relation to conscious leadership their conceptual framework of Model 1 and Model 2 as mental programmes based upon assumptions and values which we feel can be interpreted as internal cultural models that enable both anti-conscious and conscious leadership mindsets on the part of individuals.

DOI: 10.4324/9781003272793-6

Double loop learning in organisations

In his seminal article "Double Loop Learning in Organisations", published in the Harvard Business Review in 1977, Chris Argyris introduces Models 1 and 2 and their related concepts based upon empirical research into a corporation. The findings and the theory generated, which he called Double Loop Learning in Organisations, were also reproduced repeatedly based upon practical cases that Argyris and Schön (1996) researched from 1977 through to 1996 into learning errors in management teams. Their findings and subsequent theory resonate with the two authors of this book in relation to their personal experience of leading teams in organisations as well as being led. Double loop learning: learning how to learn about developing a conscious leadership culture.

The building blocks of Double Loop Learning Theory are:

- Theory in action; our authentic identity in action expressed through interactions.
- Theory of action; our ideal conception of our socially desirable identity.
- Defensive routines; techniques we use to protect our self-esteem and ego.
- Unconscious beliefs and values that limit our potential for growth.
- Single loop learning; a form of learning that simply adapts what we already know to a different situation.
- The dilemmas of power; the paradoxical nature of holding power.

When taken together, the above can explain the dynamics which generate the leadership paradox, which we shall now review.

Model 1

In many cases, aspiring leaders who are attracted to the elegance and apparent simplicity of the additive effect leadership model often cannot differentiate between their theory "of action" and their theory "in action" (Argyris, 1977). This means that they may identify logically and positively with each of the "Four Is" of the additive effect model, which is their "theory of action", i.e., their socially desirable view of themselves as ideal leaders. They may consider themselves to be transformational leaders. However, in practice, they often unconsciously adhere to an impoverished transactional leadership style, including management by exception passive or active. We use the term "impoverished" to highlight forms of transactional leadership that are not only characterised by management by exception, but they are also broadly based upon unilateral control strategies, lack of concern for developing or engaging with people, the active aim of suppressing personal and followers' emotional expressions and the framing of meaning-seeking consensus rather than dialogue. Model 1 and Model 2 as operational leadership strategies are evidenced by what the potential leaders do in action, not what they "say" they do in action. The leadership strategy they put into practice is their "theory in action". This means that human beings are capable of holding two mutually exclusive theories of influencing and, thus, leading others as they operationalise their role as leaders; the first is a fantasy construction, and the second is the authentic beliefs and values they have inculcated based upon their life experience regarding how to influence people as leaders; it is this authentic theory which Argyris refers to as their "theory in action" which drives their leadership behaviours "in practice" and creates the leadership paradox.

As Argyris and Schön (1996) imply, for Model 1 to be empirically valid, our theory of action (our espoused theory of ourselves as transformational leaders) must be influenced by another theory, our theory in action that overrides the cognitive programme supporting our theory of action. For example, a manager may claim with apparent sincerity that they always advance a participative style of leadership based on consultative engagement with followers. This would constitute their theory of action. However, when dealing with their team in a meeting concerning an organisational problem, they may, in fact, dominate airtime, rely predominantly on monologue and advance their preferred solution as the right way of going forward. They may even be intolerant of alternative perspectives or constructive feedback in relation to their framing of the problem and their preferred management solution; this would constitute their theory in action. This clear leadership paradox is an example of Model 1 in action and needs additional explanation.

Argyris and Schön (1996) put forward the idea that for Model 1 to exist, and the resulting leadership paradox to manifest, the leader must be unconsciously holding "hidden inhibiting assumptions and values". This dynamic may occur because another mental programme (our theory in action) must be deeply embedded in our unconscious mind connected to core beliefs and values we hold about the nature of human beings, and our ability to interact with influence and our values concerning personal and group development. For the lack of congruence to occur between our theory of action and our leadership behaviours in action to manifest habitually, we must be operating, unconsciously, an alternative mental programme which is "our theory in action", which can be observed as our theory in action through our actual leadership behaviours in use. This competing mindset is driving our behaviour on autopilot. It simply overrides our theory of action, our ideal version of ourselves, as it is embedded far deeper into our neurological system and is, and has been, continually validated by the selected life experiences that we acknowledge that confirm its underlying beliefs.

Model 1: a sense-making model that undermines the emergence of conscious leadership

The model 1 mindset is also one of the significant contributors towards generating staff disengagement at work either with their leaders, the organisation, the actual work or any other variable. Argyris and Schön (1996) claim that Model 1 can be the cause of low morale, withdrawal from work, lack of collaboration, poor group problem-solving skills and ineffective leadership. The reasons for this become apparent when we consider how the Model 1 mindset manifests in action.

The model 1 mindset leans towards a strategy of unilateral control out with consciousness and, as such, it is the antithesis of participative collaborative leadership/followership relationships and, thus, conscious leadership. The unconscious leader would be unaware of its existence or of its effects or causes. However, it would fully manifest in their talk and in their behaviours. The leader operating from Model 1 seeks to achieve control over human relationships and to dominate the way in which others frame social reality and behave in accordance with their imposed framings of a given situation. However, they do this in quite a sophisticated way through their use of language. For example, Argyris and Schön (1996) note that when being driven by the model 1 mindset, managers will ask questions in such a way as to get the other person to agree with their own view. Further, they will advocate their own view in a manner that limits others' questioning of it. This style of behaviour may:

1. Generate a lack of trust in groups.
2. Limit self and group learning.
3. Interfere with group resonance.
4. Create a dependency culture on the apparently omnipotent manager.
5. Hinder the self-actualisation and development of the individual members of the group.
6. Lead to poor team relationships.

When we weld the effects of Model 1 on group and individual dynamics together with an impoverished transactional leadership style either underpinned by management by exception passive or, even worse, active, then we have a powerful toxic alliance that generates negative and active disengagement/disassociation on the part of employees at multiple levels of engagement.

Model 1 is also incredibly resilient and difficult to change. When trapped in a model 1 mindset, leaders develop what Argyris (1985) refers to as "defensive routines", which they employ to protect model 1 presuppositions. Argyris (1985, p. 5) defines defensive routines as follows: "Defensive routines are thoughts and actions used to protect individuals', groups', and organizations', usual way of dealing with reality". This implies that we achieve secondary gains from adhering to our model 1 presuppositions and associated behavioural strategies even though they are incongruent with our theory of action, i.e., our socially desirable identity construction of ourselves as effective leaders. Secondary gains are defined as: "the idea that however bizzare or destructive a behaviour appears it always serves a useful purpose at some level, and this purpose is likely to be unconscious" (O'Connor and Seymour, 2011, p. 134).

For example, by not speaking up and confirming that you do not feel psycho-logically safe in the management team and that this is affecting your ability to fit in to the team, you "imagine" that you can avoid appearing in your mind, and in the minds of others, as weak. This self-protection of your identity is the secondary gain even though, paradoxically, it continues to fuel the feelings of weak internal relationships with core team members or your leader in that group. Every time we create and sustain a defensive routine that blocks self or group renewal, we do so because we achieve related secondary gains.

Another highly important effect of defensive routines, which seals Model 1 from critical reflection regarding its assumptions, reproductive strategies and reliance on related secondary gains, is a dependency on single loop learning and the diminishing potential for developing our potential for double loop learning.

Single loop learning

Argyris (1977, p. 116) defines single loop learning as follows: "When the process enables the organization to carry on its present policies or achieve its objectives, the process may be called single loop learning". This is a process of learning that draws upon established ideas and shared experiences of solv-ing operational problems. Single loop learning is associated with surface-level thinking. Single loop learning can often simply involve the retrieval of previ-ous thinking with regard to established solutions to problems. Members of a management team are introduced to the preferred organising models that have worked successfully for team members throughout their history. The underlying assumptions that previously shaped the learning are not exam-ined. This kind of learning is efficient in many cases of day-to-day problem-solving. It works productively for solving tame problems and even for critical problems. However, it does limit deep structure thinking and the emergence of leveraging the collective intelligence of the group. Also, it can solidify the power positions of the "local experts" so that only specific people from spe-cific occupations may offer solutions to specific problems. Defensive routines can also be used to block the entrance of new ideas and methods of solv-ing organisational problems, such as dialogue circles with statements such as "don't use any jargon", or "keep the language simple", which is basically code for "no learning takes place here other than single loop learning". As words are vehicles for concepts and conduits for learning, then censoring the words managers can use censors knowledge acquisition and inhibits organisational learning in terms of double loop learning; i.e., the kind of learning required to solve wicked problems such as creating a conscious leadership culture as a replacement to an impoverished transactional leadership culture.

Double loop learning

Double loop learning involves teaching or encouraging people to think more deeply about their own assumptions and beliefs; this is central to conscious leadership. This involves accessing deep structure thinking (O'Connor and Seymour, 2011), which involves active and conscious reflexivity (Alvesson et al., 2017) towards the unconscious basis for the validity of a proposed single loop learning solution and the beliefs and values that support it. It aims to solve a wicked problem, for example, transforming an impoverished transactional leadership culture supported by a shared model 1 mindset into a thriving enriching model of transactional or transformational leadership enabled through a conscious leadership mindset characterised by model 2 values, beliefs and behavioural strategies in use.

Model 2: a sense-making model that enables the emergence of a conscious leadership mindset

Drawing from the ideas of Argyris and Schön (1996), we can see that the main difference between Model 1 and Model 2 as problem-solving and influencing mindsets is that Model 1 is based on single loop learning protected by defensive routines enabled by unilateral social control strategies whilst Model 2 is based upon double loop learning, the minimisation of defensive routines, or at least the public outing of these, and, of course, deep structure thinking. Based, again, on the work of Argyris and Schön (1996), leaders who have adopted a model 2 mindset exhibit the following behavioural strategies:

1. They are interested in the rationale behind others' views.
2. They advocate their own view and reasoning in a way that encourages others to confront it and to help the speaker discover where the view may be mistaken.
3. They state, publicly, the inferences that they make and encourage reflection.
4. They aim to generate valid information and informed choice.
5. They aim to achieve internal commitment from the group behind the choices made with regard to solving problems.
6. They adopt bilateral strategies for co-operation and participation.
7. They encourage and practice reflexivity.
8. They are perceptually flexible and can work comfortably with open, differentiated and integrated perspective-taking and are not prisoners of their own closed perspective.

There are clear similarities between a conscious leadership mindset and a model 2 mindset. However, the significant distinction is that a conscious leadership mindset aims to facilitate reflexivity towards our:

- Emotional strategies in use.
- Cognitive strategies in use.
- Behavioural strategies in use.
- Linguistic strategies in use.

- The beliefs and values and life experiences that influence the choices of strategy we make.
- Defensive strategies in use.

Conscious leadership is the state of being (Anderson and Anderson, 2010) supported by specific methods of intervention that enable the transition from a model 1 to model 2 mindset through a process of purposeful awakening and intervention and change management.

An example of double loop learning

Double loop learning, as an example, could be reflecting upon our theory of action, identifying and describing our leadership behaviours in action and pinpointing the discrepancy and effects on leadership/follower dynamics. Thus, we need a tool for identifying our core operating system that is driving our presentation of self as leaders in our theory in action. This tool is called "reflexivity" (Alvesson et al., 2017) and is at the very heart of the conscious leadership paradigm. Reflexivity refers to the critical examination of one's own beliefs, judgments and practices during the leadership/management process and how these may have influenced the leadership/follower dynamic. This process also involves identifying primary and secondary inhibiting loops.

Primary and secondary inhibiting loops

The adherence to Model 1 is reinforced by a network of primary and secondary inhibiting loops which also serve to block double loop learning (Argyris, 1977). For example, a tendency to keep deep structure discussion regarding the organisational problems of the table and to reduce sense-making to surface level reductionist monologues serves as a primary inhibiting loop that blocks differentiated perspective-taking regarding the actual nature of a problem. This primary inhibiting loop then interacts with the model 1 preference of advocating a closed framing of perspective towards a given situation. It also ensures that other alternatives and possible fruitful framing of the problem and its causes are blocked. Finally, it ensures that the competency of the leader and their teams to move with emotional intelligence through the range of possible learning perspectives, e.g., closed to open, to differentiated, to integrated, is stunted.

The primary inhibiting loop will also generate secondary inhibiting loops which serve to reinforce and insulate the primary inhibiting loop from interference and change. For example, if a manager questions the framing of a problem, they may be censored from the meeting. They may be gently mocked by colleagues for rocking the boat and for being "controversial", followed up by some "friendly" advice to stick to script in the future. This is an example of a secondary inhibiting loop, i.e., peer group censorship supporting a primary inhibiting loop, e.g., framing problems superficially from a closed perspective which then supports Model 1, the manager's right for advocacy to frame the definition of a problem.

The dilemmas of power

The above challenges also represent dilemmas of power for leaders that are exemplified by problems identified by Argyris (1977, p. 123), such as:

1. How to be strong, yet admit the existence of dilemmas.
2. How to behave openly, yet not be controlling.
3. How to advocate and still encourage confrontation of their views.
4. How to respond effectively to subordinates' anxieties in spite of their own.
5. How to manage fear, yet ask people to overcome their fears and become more open.
6. How to gain credibility for attempts to change their leadership style when they are not comfortable with such a style.

The above challenges are complex and demanding. The solution, we feel, lies within a conscious leadership mindset and related practices to help facilitate the transitional process of managing the leadership paradox with conscious awareness, which involves:

- Managing a transition from an impoverished transactional mindset to an enriching alternative mindset.
- Managing the transition from a model 1 to a model 2 operating programme.
- Responding to dilemmas of power in a resourceful way.
- Identifying then deconstructing and reducing the significance of primary and secondary inhibiting loops.

Conclusion

The ability to recognise when a management team is stuck in a model 1 mindset requires an awareness of the key ideas outlined throughout this chapter. However, recognition is one part of the conscious leadership process; the awakening leadership team also need to move towards acceptance of this mindset. Acceptance involves assuming personal responsibility for the internalisation and habitualisation of a model 1 mindset and for its leadership effects on staff engagement, participation and organisational learning. This is not a process that happens over a space of a short two- to three-hour workshop. Rather, it is a gradual process of awakening involving 360-degree feedback, staff surveys, focus groups and one-to-one interviews, as well as action learning workshops with the management team. This process also needs to be facilitated by a skilled conscious leadership coach. The transition from Model

1 to Model 2 would benefit from individual, group and intergroup coaching. This is a leadership process that targets a wicked problem. In the next chapter, we will explore this process of conscious leadership awakening in more detail.

References

Alvesson, M., Blom, M. & Sveninssson, S. (2017) *Reflexive Leadership: Organising in an Imperfect World.* Sage.

Anderson, D. & Anderson, L. (2010) *Beyond Change Management: How to Achieve Breakthrough Results Through Conscious Change Leadership.* John Wiley and Sons.

Argyris, C. (1977) Double Loop Learning in Organizations. *Harvard Business Review.*

Argyris, C. (1985) *Strategy, Change, and Defensive Routines.* Pitman.

Argyris, C. & Schön, D.A. (1996) *Organizational Learning II: Theory, Method and Practice.* Addison Wesley.

O'Connor, J. & Seymour, J. (2011) *Introducing NLP: Psychological Skills for Understanding and Influencing People.* HarperCollins.

6 AWAKENING THE NEED FOR CHANGE

Introduction

A fundamental act of leadership is what Alvesson et al. (2017) refer to as "everyday reframing" or what Dilts (2003) calls "awakening". This process, for example, may involve eliciting in leadership prospects an introspective mindset to identify behavioural, emotional and/or cognitive strategies and their associated beliefs and values that generate impoverished leadership styles and weaken follower/leadership engagement dynamics. This chapter explores this awakening process and identifies some key organisational factors, such as the idea of "managing in the moment" (Parker, 2013) and connects these with the dominant model of transactional leadership. The idea that culture produces leadership style (Schein, 1985) is discussed, inclusive of its function in reproducing leadership styles. Thereafter, the difficult conundrum of triggering reflexivity within a leadership team to explore the nature of their leadership culture and consider changing aspects of its form is explored. Finally, we review action research as a fundamental aspect of organisational development (OD) (French and Bell, 1999) and illustrate, by example, how an action research strategy rooted in corporate governance can act as an awakening tool to enable conscious leadership practices based upon reflexivity and survey feedback.

Transactional leadership suits managing in the moment

It seems to be common sense that the world of organisation requires transactional leadership in order to work effectively and achieve its day-to-day operational goals. It also appears to be common sense that transformational leadership involves an extraordinary form of leadership influence which energises followers and leaders to achieve standards of performance that are also extraordinary. However, it is the day-to-day management of organisations that seems to dominate management thinking and acting. The practice of transcending day-to-day nitty-gritty operational management and leaning into the future (Williams and Binney, 1997), doing work today to build an organisation that is fit for the future, and a future that may be beyond the employment history of many managers, seems to be uncommon.

DOI: 10.4324/9781003272793-7

As a result of the pressing need to manage in the moment and not think strategically, the dominant model of leadership is transactional. This phenomenon has been described as "strategic myopia" (Mazzarol et al., 2010). This is a significant issue that will contribute towards the steady and gradual decline of the organisation's health and its ability to master its trading environment. This is because the trading environment is continually changing, and there is a danger that the organisation will simply slip into a strategic drift and find itself unaligned with its environment. The form of the dominant leadership style will also produce the cultural norms of the organisation that will sustain either a model 1 or model 2 mindset within the management team. It is established in literature that leadership style informs culture, which then reproduces and sustains leadership style (Schein, 1985).

Leadership style generates cultural style

A not so insignificant barrier to the awakening and transition process towards conscious leadership is an organisational culture that may also be toxic. By toxic, we mean that the beliefs and values that are impeding organisational learning are taught to newcomers, encourage and sustain an impoverished transactional leadership culture and a model 1 mindset associated with single loop learning and its supporting defensive routines. A form of unconscious bias may creep in which ensures that leadership appointments are those individuals who "fit in" to the established way of doing things. This form of bias is known as affinity bias (Davies, 2018). This strategy may work when you have an organisation characterised by model 2 mental programmes and growth mindsets underpinned by transactional management styles that are enriching and reflective, perhaps even involving elements of coaching. However, when the organisational culture is based upon a model 1 mindset, expressed through an impoverished transactional leadership style based upon both dissociated relationships between leaders and staff and management by exception active, then it can be understood to be both a toxic culture and have the status of a declining organisation (Merry and Brown, 1988).

This phenomenon we can usefully refer to as "anti-conscious leadership" (Bowman and Bowman, 2014). Anti-conscious leaders are those leaders who actively work against the consciousness awakening in themselves and those around them and who work hard at creating and maintaining their ethnocentric version of reality. They are not sensitive to the need to share information and tend to create a CRASH state in themselves and in others. Bowman and Bowman (2014) also note that anti-conscious leaders tend to work purely from a closed perspective (Dixon, 1998) and have a strong motivation to debate and win the argument, a process of communication that is anti-empathy and anti-curiosity and leans heavily towards sustaining a model 1 mindset. It is important to acknowledge the idea, though, that anti-conscious leaders are not considered to be a certain kind of person. People are not their behaviour;

rather, their behaviours are a product of their mindset, and their mindset is a process of sense-making filtered through values and beliefs (Dweck, 2012). Thus, mindset is a social construction that is always in process and open to enforcement or change (Hardy, 2020).

The presence of anti-conscious leadership as a group phenomenon signifies that the leadership culture of an organisation is characterised by a lack of individual and group reflexivity and an enthusiastic rejection of the principles of double loop learning. Behaviours, attitudes and emotions are expressly operated on autopilot as they are being driven by culturally modelled mental programmes that lie deep within our unconscious mind (Hofstede et al., 2010). These mental programmes have been referred to as cultural themes, a concept now firmly established within anthropology. Cultural themes were defined by anthropologist Morris Opler (1945, p. 198) as: "A postulate or position, declared or implied, and usually controlling behaviour or stimulating activity, which is tacitly approved or openly promoted in a society". Cultural themes can operate as powerful and efficient defensive routines (McCalman and Potter, 2015).

An example of a cultural theme that can operate unchallenged in an organisation with an anti-conscious leadership culture is one that may assert that a position that management development, based on formal study within a business school, is a wasteful activity with no real practical benefits. This reflects a model 1 mindset. This cultural theme advances the belief shared by managers that management and/or leadership development is a practical affair conducted through practical experience. What has worked in the past is often highly valued and it is assumed that these approaches will continue to work in the future. This belief system also acts as a filter for training and recruiting emerging leaders and for managing management talent. This organic talent management strategy does not include external agencies such as business schools. This is clearly a theme that promotes anti-learning.

Opler (1945) asserts that there will be a limited number of cultural themes in use, and these will dominate the expressive content and capacity of a group. This means that to understand the cultural forces that provide the roots to a model 1 mindset and an impoverished transactional leadership culture, which we define as anti-conscious leadership, we need to unpack the cultural themes in use, and this involves qualitative research methods such as participant observation, survey feedback, focus groups and one-to-one interviews (Spradley, 1980).

Conversely, to understand the cultural roots that support a model 2 mindset expressed through a nourishing transactional leadership culture which we define as conscious leadership, once again, the method of understanding would involve cultural theme analysis. For example, in a conscious leadership culture, a cultural theme in use could be the ritual of managers when starting a team meeting accessing a group COACH state to bring individual presence to the meeting and to access the collective intelligence of the group mediated through enabling thinking styles, behaviours, attitude's and emotions (Dilts, 2017). This ritual is based upon the cultural theme that advocates the position that individual and group state management activities that are based on mindfulness generate high-quality leadership interactions.

The most difficult part of conscious leadership is for senior leaders to untangle these cultural dynamics, present the cultural themes that support anti-conscious leadership behaviours that need intervention and secure the agreement of their senior team towards the intervention, which involves the creation of new resourceful cultural themes that support a conscious leadership culture. This involves facing up to and acknowledging the constraining impact on reflexivity caused by cultural hegemony (McCalman and Potter, 2015).

Cultural hegemony

Cultural hegemony can be understood as a system of soft power based upon a network of cultural themes that have no counterweight and, thus, morph into what is effectively a system of themes that stand over and suffocate any new form of cultural expression (Chomsky, 1992). Hegemony is primarily concerned with social construction processes. Hegemony retains its distinctiveness as a form of soft power because it is based upon socio/ideological control rather than blunt coercive mechanisms. As a form of socio/ideological control, hegemony is effective because it aims to influence social construction processes. Therefore, hegemony, at a primary level, is concerned with both the social construction of reality on the part of actors to advance their sectional interests and to culturally reproduce existing power relations (Bourdieu, 1991).

Hegemony is defined by Humphreys and Brown (2002) as deriving from its use by Gramsci (1971), which refers to an ideology that is so deeply embedded in a culture that it is taken as natural. Hegemony, in this sense, is primarily understood as a means of cultural domination to privilege the interests of the ruling elite. Humphreys and Brown (2002, p. 423) cite Clegg's (1989) description of hegemony as: "Hegemony thus involves the successful mobilisation and reproduction of the active consent of dominated groups". The power of hegemony, according to Boje et al. (2004), is based on its ability to control the expressive capacity of actors to construct their own interpretation of desired social realities.

For example, if unchecked, a cultural theme of anti-learning will become hegemonic because, as it is unchallenged, it becomes so deeply embedded in the mindset of members that it is taken for granted as the normal way of things. Or, the cultural theme of leaders applying unilateral control strategies as core interactive strategies with team members becomes hegemonic when it exists unchallenged and is treated as normative. It can even be the case that a manager who tries to employ bilateral interactive sense-making to arrive at shared decisions and definitions of situations may be perceived to be dysfunctional, weird or disruptive as they are mismatching the normative cultural theme of unilateral control over defining reality and acting on these definitions.

It is often the case that when a manager introduces new ideas that they face resistance from their more established colleagues. This defensive culture is arguably the common cold of dysfunctional learning cultures and blocks the emergence of the learning organisation (Senge, 1990). These responses, as previously discussed, are called defensive routines (Argyris and Schön, 1974).

We must understand that managers who behave in a way that blocks personal and group learning may do so because they feel insecure and vulnerable and by opening up and revealing this and their ignorance can be a distinctive threat to their self-image. Hegemony, as a form of expressive control and domination, targets expressions, whether these are linguistic, conceptual, behavioural, identity or knowledge. Anti-conscious leadership cultures are essentially hegemonic structures protected by a system of defensive routines and primary and secondary inhibiting loops.

To lead a successful transition from anti-conscious leadership culture to one that is characterised by a conscious leadership culture that is crafting an organisation that will be fit for the future is an act of transformational leadership involving cultural change and, inevitably, will challenge hegemonic structures. This is a cultural change project involving double loop learning. The project aims to change the underlying beliefs and values that produce the cultural themes in use that support a model 1 mindset expressed through an impoverished transactional leadership model, which manifests as an anti-conscious leadership culture. This transformation is required to adopt alternative enabling beliefs and values that generate the adoption of a model 2 mindset and a nourishing transactional leadership model with the potential of embedding transformational leadership resources throughout the wider leadership network within the organisation at large. The first part of this transformational project concerns awakening the need for change, which involves a classic wicked problem that we refer to as a leadership conundrum (Lawler and Gold, 2016).

A leadership conundrum

The elephant in the room when it comes to the established change leadership literature concerns a leadership conundrum: *"How do we know what we do not know we need to know in order to be more effective leaders in our organisations?"* This is a question of personal and group awakening. The seeds of an answer to this conundrum potentially lie within another question which is: *"What is the standard and quality of staff engagement in this organisation?"* The quality of staff engagement is a key performance indicator with regard to the quality and effectiveness of organisational leadership and the general health of the organisation at large.

This is not a new issue facing leadership teams. Blake and McCanse (1991) argue, persuasively, that it was not access to material or economic or technological resources that generated sustainable organisational success; rather, it was how leaders managed their cognitive, behavioural and emotional resources through their interactions with followers to establish quality engagement standards. Blake and McCanse (1991, p. 4) claim that:

> Sometimes we observe very talented people who don't produce the results we expect. Frequently, the reason for this is faulty relationships. Such is the case of a person who appears to have great resources at his or her disposal but is repeatedly unable to establish constructive relationships with those who must help produce the results. Often the solution lies in recognising the adverse consequences of one's leadership – those things a person does that negatively impact others or those things a person fails to do that, if done, could prove to be beneficial.

Their work into improving leadership/follower dynamics has been highly influential within the OD field and is arguably based upon the idea of raising the conscious awareness of leaders with regard to their leadership style and how that impacts the quality of follower relationships. They conclude that:

> The key to greater productivity lies in recognizing these adverse consequences of leadership. Once people have an objective view of how they operate, change towards more effective behaviour becomes an option. In other words, if we continue to do things – of which we are often unaware – that adversely affect teamwork and organization productivity, little or no change can occur. We must be able to see and diagnose our weaknesses in order to move toward a sounder way of operating. We must also be able to see our strengths so we can reinforce them.

Blake and McCanse (1991) are clearly calling for the development of reflexivity capabilities in leaders (Alvesson et al., 2017). They implicitly acknowledge that, in many cases, leaders and, indeed, leadership teams may be in a state of unconscious incompetence regarding their reflexive skills, and the role of organisational development practitioners working with these leadership groups is to raise their awareness of this weakness and move the leaders through a process of personal and group awakening that generates personal development and group learning, resulting in a highly reflexive leadership team. Blake and McCanse (1991) were implicitly calling for a transition towards conscious leadership based upon qualitative research to enable reflexivity. Detailed below is an action research strategy we have used successfully to enable this reflexive transition towards conscious leadership practices within a leadership team.

Action research

At the heart of the organisational development movement lies the applied practice of action research. Organisational development (OD) is defined by French and Bell (1999, p. 26) as: "A long-term effort supported by top management to improve an organization's visioning, empowerment, learning, and problem-solving processes through an ongoing, collaborative management of organizational culture – using the consultant-facilitator role and the theory and technology of applied behavioural science, including action research". This definition emphasises the relationship between practice and conceptual models of organisational development. OD can be considered as an applied field of practice that is action-orientated and underpinned by theory. OD was, and remains, an approach to organisational change that frames the organisation as an open social and cultural system. It assumes that an interrelationship exists between human behaviours, interactions and organisational performance. It aims towards increasing the behavioural, cognitive and emotive flexibility of leaders in organisations to generate highly productive leadership/followership relationships.

The OD movement was originally founded in the late 1940s by behavioural change pioneers such as Kurt Lewin, Ronald Lippitt, Kenneth Benne and Leland Bradford. Together with their followers, they designed action research programmes targeting group change work in both community and organisational settings. They were influenced by the psychotherapist Carl Rogers (1951) and his ideas of client-centred therapy. The pioneers initially referred to themselves as "trainers", establishing a network of "National Training Laboratories" (NTLs) throughout the USA. Organisational development action learning sets spread throughout the world due to collaborative partnerships between the original pioneers and colleagues such as Robert Trist at the Tavistock Institute in the UK. The main emphasis was on developing action research agendas. The primary setting for the NTLs was to be faculties located within forward thinking business schools. The purpose was to develop a body of theory and practice which could be used by practitioners, supported by OD consultants, trained and educated in the behavioural sciences, to work intelligently from an evidence base on organisational change projects.

Action research and the conscious leadership coach

Action Research (AR) is the building block of OD. French and Bell (1999, p. 130) define action research as: "The process of systematically collecting research data about an ongoing system relative to some objective, goal, or need of that system; feeding these data back into the system; taking actions by altering selected variables within the system based both on the data and on hypothesis; and evaluating the results of actions by collecting more data". A typical action research project would involve gathering valid data that would inform leadership thinking and trigger reflexivity and introspection with regard to everyone's contribution to the established leadership culture and its dynamics, especially staff engagement and disengagement outcomes. The action research process is a linear process that starts with reflexivity and making sense of the need for change. This is followed by the applied research process to gather research data. The data, once gathered, would then be distilled down into accessible themes and, from the findings, suggestions for change would be made. The precise nature of the interventions would then be agreed upon and implemented. Finally, the impact of the implementation on the management culture would be reflected upon and any modifications to the intervention actioned.

Conclusion

Leaders cannot change a corporate culture that lacks conscious leadership unless they change the established language in use. This can only happen through a process of dialogical exchange between team members. This awakening process is one based upon action research and action learning. It is a highly reflexive process guided by well-formed and relevant research questions. Its aim is to generate valid data or information and to engage in open participation based on free will on the part of the leadership team. It must be facilitated by trained coaches who are schooled in OD and understand behavioural science and personal and group development techniques. Moving from a culture of unconscious transactional leadership based on Model 1 and single loop learning to a culture of conscious leadership based on Model 2 and double loop learning is a significant change project. It requires careful thought and a serious investment in time and leadership commitment. It also involves challenging the status quo and challenging, and even disrupting, established power relationships and, thus, may involve the management of conflict as well as the management of collaboration catalysts. Fundamentally, this is an act of conscious leadership. It requires intelligent change management based on a comprehensive understanding of leadership models inclusive of anti-conscious leadership, the dynamics of which we turn our attention to in the chapter that follows.

References

Alvesson, M., Blom, M. & Sveningsson, S. (2017) *Reflexive Leadership: Organising in an Imperfect World*. Sage.

Argyris, C. & Schön, D.A. (1974) *Theory in Practice: Increasing Professional Effectiveness*. Jossey-Bass.

Blake, R. & McCanse, A. (1991) *Leadership Dilemmas – Grid Solutions*. Management and Organization Development Series. Blake/Mouton Grid.

Boje, M.D., Oswick, C. & Ford, D.J. (2004) Language and Organisation: The Doing of Discourse. *Academy of Management Review*, 4, pp. 571–577.

Bourdieu, P. (1991) *Language and Symbolic Capital*. Polity Press.

Bowman, S. & Bowman, C. (2014) *Conscious Leadership: The Key to Unlocking Success*. Access Consciousness Publishing Company.

Clegg, S. (1989) *Frameworks of Power*. Sage.

Chomsky, N. (1992) *Deferring Democracy*. Vintage.

Davies, J.R. (2018) *7 Ways Unconscious Bias Impacts Your Daily Interactions at Work*. https://insights.learnlight.com/en/articles/unconscious-bias-impacts-work/.

Dilts, R. (2003) *From Coach to Awakener*. Meta Publications.

Dilts, R. (2017) *Conscious Leadership and Resilience*. Dilts Strategy Group.

Dixon, N.M. (1998) *Dialogue at Work*. Lemos & Crane.

Dweck, C.S. (2012) *Mindset: How You Can Fulfil Your Potential*. Constable & Robinson.

French, L.W. & Bell, H.C. (1999) *Organization Development: Behavioral Science Interventions for Organization Improvement*. Prentice-Hall.

Gramsci, A. (1971) *Selections from the Prison Notebooks*. Lawrence and Wishart.

Hardy, B. (2020) *Personality Isn't Permanent: Break Free from Self-Limiting Beliefs and Rewrite Your Story*. Penguin.

Hofstede, G., Hofstede, G.J. & Minkov, M. (2010) *Cultures and Organizations: Software of the Mind: Intercultural Cooperation and Its Importance for Survival*. McGraw-Hill.

Humphreys, M. & Brown, A.D. (2002) Narratives of Organisational Identity and Identification: A Case Study of Hegemony and Resistance. *Organisation Studies*, 3, 41–449.

Lawler, J. & Gold, J. (2016) The Leader's Conundrum: A Paradox of Distortion. In: *Leadership Paradoxes: Rethinking Leadership for an Uncertain World*. Taylor & Francis, pp. 93–113.

Mazzarol, T. (2010) Do you suffer from strategic myopia? *Center for Entrepreneurial Management and Innovation* 11/9/2010 [Blog]. Available at https://cemi.com.au/node/91

McCalman, J. & Potter, D. (2015) *Leading Cultural Change: The Theory and Practice of Successful Organizational Transformation*. Kogan Page.

Merry, U. & Brown, L.G. (1988) *The Neurotic Behavior of Organizations*. Gardner Press.

Opler, M. (1945) Themes as Dynamic Forces in Culture. *American Journal of Sociology*, 53, pp. 198–206.

Parker, L. (2013) *Managing the Moment: A Leader's Guide to Building Executive Presence One Interaction at a Time*. Advantage Media Group.

Rogers, C.R. (1951) *Client-Centred Therapy*, Kindle edn. Constable & Robinson.

Schein, H.E. (1985) *Organisational Culture and Leadership*. Jossey- Bass Publishers.

Senge, M.P. (1990) The *Fifth Discipline: The Art and Practice of the Learning Organization*. Doubleday/Currency.

Spradley, P.J. (1980) *Participant Observation*. Wadsworth.

Williams, C. & Binney, G. (1997) *Leaning into the Future Changing the Way People Change Organizations*. Nicholas Brealey Pub.

7 THE DYNAMICS OF ANTI-CONSCIOUS LEADERSHIP EXPLORED

Introduction

We need a model of anti-conscious leadership that is coherent and accessible to managers and one that can be used as a reflexive and diagnostic tool. The aim is to support managers with conscious leadership potential through their reflexive process without judging them. All behaviours have positive intentions (O'Connor and Seymour, 2011), and, often, we act in unreflective ways; when acting in the moment, we are unaware of other choices we can make regarding our interactive styles. It can also be the case that our interactive styles are "unconsciously modelled", drawing on role models who are selected as our significant others that are culturally signified as successful and effective in an organisation (Mead, 1934). Thus, there is often no counterpoint in a management culture that exhibits the characteristics of anti-conscious leadership.

The awakening process is a clear example of leadership efforts to act with conscious leadership, and the associated organisational double loop learning process requires tools to maximise the opportunities for personal and group development offered throughout the awakening. Having a clear understanding of what creates a culture of anti-conscious leadership and which sustains a reliance on Model 1 and single loop learning, and their associated defensive routines, is of enormous practical value. Therefore, this chapter unpacks the interrelated elements of our anti-conscious leadership model and explains their dynamics. To start this exploration, we initially explore leadership membership exchange theory as a conceptual backdrop to the wider discussion regarding anti-conscious leadership elements.

Leadership membership exchange theory

Leader membership exchange theory (LMX) has been defined by Peter Northouse (2010, p. 147) as: "*A theory that conceives leadership as a process that is focused on the interactions between leaders and their followers*". The principle behind LMX as a theory is that the leadership/follower dynamic emerges from

DOI: 10.4324/9781003272793-8

resourceful relationships between the leadership and follower prospects. The research focus on understanding leadership/followership dynamics should, therefore, be orientated towards the micro interactive sense-making process and associated behaviours and emotional expressions. What people do and how they do it in terms of emotive, cognitive and behavioural intra- and inter-personal interactions matters considerably if one is to understand leadership and followers and build an engaged, high-performance conscious leadership culture. LMX emphasises relationships and the quality of the leadership/follower relationship dynamics. This implies that social and cultural flexibility should be considered fundamental, practical leadership competencies, with reflexivity central to forging such a competency. This means that conscious leaders should be practising, with awareness, new behavioural, emotional and cognitive interactive strategies. LMX theory rejects a standard generic leadership strategy based on command and control.

LMX is focused upon the dyadic relationship between a leadership prospect and a follower prospect (Graen and Uhl-Bien, 1995). This one-to-one relationship is where the sense-making and interactions occur that either create strong leadership/followership or weak leadership/followership relationships. The logic is that it is the sum of the quality of dyadic leadership/followership relationships that produces the quality and strength of the leadership team. The dyadic relationship enables the quality of the leadership influence.

LMX is also known for the distinction the theory makes between "in- and out-group team members" (Breukelen et al., 2006). What often happens is that leaders attract those they feel most at ease with as "in-group" members and place those they find different, or perhaps challenging, in their "out-group". The in-group enjoy the leader's sponsorship and have greater political influence over the out-group. They have more voice and, usually, will enjoy greater unofficial privileges and access to self-actualising opportunities. The out-group, by comparison, will be relatively marginalised, lack political influence and be treated with more formality; they will be exposed to interactions that are somewhat dissociated socially from the leader and the in-group members.

Fundamental examples of conceptual elements of LMX are the dyad, the in-group and the out-group. The dyad is the pairing of a leader and a member of their team. The in-group are those team members with whom a leader enjoys high levels of rapport. The out-group are those team members whom the leader has a weak rapport with. These three identity constructs arguably form the basis of leadership teams. Any attempt to transform the nature of a leadership culture must take as its unit of analysis and change the beliefs and values that underpin the quality and style of relationships and interactions that form the basis of leadership membership exchange in all three categories of identity constructs.

Changing organisational culture such as targeting a transactional leadership culture and moving towards a conscious leadership culture is a clear example of a wicked problem. The principles of LMX theory are incredibly useful as they illuminate the need to focus in upon the micro social and political interactions that drive the belief and value system within the management community. This focus of change is often not adopted when management groups attempt to change their leadership culture. The need to be critically self-reflexive as a leader and to identify within yourself a need to change the way you relate to your team members and be open to critical evaluation from them is an emotionally challenging affair. The emerging conscious leader needs to feel psychologically safe if they are to be fully available psychologically for such a learning and personal development journey. This means that organisations need to provide the support to enable such a state of psychological safety to emerge and to do this they need to both understand the concept and value its potential benefits. Techniques such as mentoring and coaching are highly effective as supportive resources for this kind of wicked problem.

Many leaders are embedded between both in- and out-group members. The key driver of in-group leadership relationships is "personal compatibility", which involves rapport, close social relationships and trust, which generate regular and high levels of social interactions. In contrast, the out-group members have more formal relationships with their leadership prospects. According to LMX, leaders operate from associated states towards in-group members and disassociated states with out-group members.

A key strength of LMX is that it challenges leaders to be reflexive with regard to their relationships with all individual team members, whether they are in- or out-group members, with the aim of eliminating the out-group phenomenon and establishing a coherent and integrated high performing team based upon associated behaviours, positive identifications, rapport and mutual respect between each individual. As a leader, increasing one's awareness and understanding of the value of building and sustaining high levels of rapport with all individuals through critical reflection will contribute towards greater personal, team and organisational success (Potter, 2018).

LMX also places emphasis upon the principle of exchange between leaders and followers, particularly within the in-group, which may involve, as stated above, access to traditionally valued personal and organisational resources and opportunities for growth and development; thus, enjoying a potent mix of extrinsic and intrinsic motivators whilst the out-group may be restricted to low-level extrinsic motivators such as their salary and similar normative rewards. This means that the LMX inspired model of leadership is fundamentally based upon transactionalism that emphasises that all co-operation is based upon expected exchanges and rewards. This is the essence of the LMX dyadic relationship. Both leaders and followers receive rewards from each other, and it is this sense of mutual reciprocity that oils LMX relationships. The model, however, contains the seeds of decline and decay.

The out-group element of the leadership team is always a source of tension and unhappiness that, through time, can magnify and flow over into open inter-group conflicts. The leader may retreat into more excessive, dissociated and formal strategies to manage relationships with out-group members. This dynamic will upset relations with and between in-group members also. If the leader has provided the in-group members with too much social access and power, they may also not be able to exercise quality influence over them as a leader and splits may appear in the in-group, creating in-groups within in-groups. This process of team decay can lead to high levels of distrust, lack of rapport and, ultimately, weak leadership dynamics across both in- and out-groups. This situation gets out of control if the leader is stuck in a model 1 mindset and relies upon single loop learning and actively practices defensive routines resulting in a lack of reflexivity and social and cultural flexibility in terms of the strategies they have access to.

The idea of flexible strategies explored

Central to our book is the idea that the emotions we generate, the behaviours we exhibit and the attitudes that are implicit in our thinking can be considered as our "social strategies", which generate our social results. We frame a situation based upon the meanings that we attribute to the contents of that situation; then, we select, either consciously or unconsciously, the social strategies we assume are correct for the situation. In every social situation, we hold the view that people always make the best decision they can make, allowing for the resources that they have and their awareness of choice (O'Connor and Seymour, 2011). Therefore, by accepting the idea that if we bring anger, defensive body language and a critical mindset to a meeting, we have chosen these social strategies. If these strategies support an anti-conscious leadership culture, then they have been both habitualised and modelled.

However, it is critical that we bear in mind that all cultural norms and their associated beliefs and values are social constructions of our own making (Schein, 1985). Our leaders in the past have created these cultural norms; their prodigies model these and then reproduce them. This means that whatever aspect of culture we socially construct, we can socially deconstruct and that we have the power to design the leadership culture we all wish to belong to (McCalman and Potter, 2015). In Figure 7.1, we introduce our model of

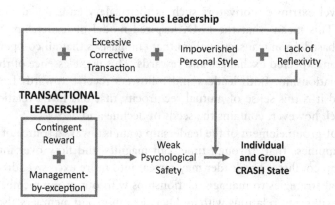

Figure 7.1 Anti-conscious Leadership

anti-conscious leadership which illustrates some of the main blockers of a conscious leadership culture emerging in an organisation.

Building rapport

Building rapport with followers is a fundamental conscious leadership competency as well as a core coaching capability. Rapport has been defined by O'Connor and Seymour (2011, p. 234) as: "The process of establishing and maintaining a relationship of mutual trust and understanding between two or more people". We have all experienced being in a state of rapport with individuals or groups. There is usually a feeling of being accepted by the others, not being judged, relaxed, open and easy in their company. We may feel a strong sense of connection. Our body language may match those we are in rapport with, as does our energy. We may feel that the other is interested in our perspectives and is sympathetic regarding our views and interpretation of our experiences. There will be a high level of trust.

Rapport as a state is characterised by low resistance between two or more individuals and enables alignment of values, attitudes, beliefs and behaviours. Rapport is based upon mutual trust, confidence and acceptance. Dembkowski et al. (2006, p. 22) advance the premise that rapport is the essence of close communication between the coach and the client and that it forms the foundation of any coaching conversation. Furthermore, coaching, either self-coaching or with the help of a specialist coach, to win our "inner game" (Gallwey, 1999) is an essential conscious leadership resource and skill set (Dilts, 2017). Personable warmth, active listening, non-judgementalism, understanding, empathising and connecting are key characteristics that should bond the conscious leadership/follower relationship together. The rapport-building model commonly used in coaching and leadership situations (O'Connor and Seymour, 2011) is illustrated in Figure 7.2.

Calibrating involves reading the emotional, cognitive and behavioural states of others and of ourselves. Pacing is defined by O'Connor and Seymour (2011, p. 233) as: "Gaining and maintaining rapport with another person over a period of time by joining them in their model of the world. You can pace beliefs as well as behaviours". Matching involves reflecting the body language, emotional and cognitive states and cultural models demonstrated in the other. When managed fluently, these three elements can lead to strong rapport between leaders and followers and, thus, can generate authentic and reliable leadership outcomes.

Weak rapport

When rapport is weak, we experience quite different states. We may feel tense, uneasy, uncertain regarding the other; we may be defensive and feel that our identity or capabilities are being judged. We may feel disconnected, separate and dissociated from the other. Our body language may mismatch that of the

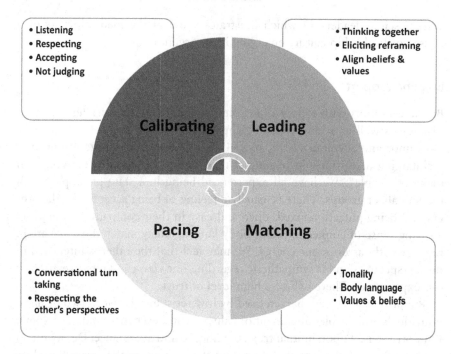

- Listening
- Respecting
- Accepting
- Not judging

- Thinking together
- Eliciting reframing
- Align beliefs & values

Calibrating   **Leading**

Pacing   **Matching**

- Conversational turn taking
- Respecting the other's perspectives

- Tonality
- Body language
- Values & beliefs

Figure 7.2 Rapport-building Model

other's, as will our energy, both in style and intensity. We may feel that the other is not interested in our perspectives and even may be harshly critical of these. They may not show any evidence of wishing to pace or understand our experience. We may even feel quite anxious and insecure. There will be a lack of trust.

To help us bring some life to our anti-conscious leadership model, we shall use a short case study to illuminate its fundamental elements.

The project director

Charles was in his mid-fifties. He was a highly experienced executive who had held senior management roles for most of his 30-year career. Charles was seen as a "doer" and manager who got things done. He was very task-orientated and emphasised profit as the main indicator of success. Charles had flourished in a company that was known throughout its industry as an aggressive operator that maximised profit and related productivity themes. The company traded in high-volume, high-margin sectors. Charles held a short-term operational view and was not inclined to operate strategically or invest in either his own personal development or that of his staff. The culture Charles presided over was incredibly hierarchical.

The company had a management training programme which was called "Modern Leadership Apprentices". They hired young graduates as MLA Trainees who spent at least six months in various departments under the management of an assigned leadership role model over a three-year period to "learn the business". They were paid a salary based on minimum wage and were expected to work long hours with no overtime payments. Their progression through the apprentice programme was driven by six monthly reviews composed by their leadership role models. The turnover of the leadership apprentices was very high, and those that did complete the programme were promoted to Junior Assistant Trainee Managers, and, again, their career progression was based on six monthly reviews. As they successfully progressed following positive reviews, their job was redefined and their job title edited to signify greater status, e.g., from Junior Assistant Trainee Manager to Assistant Trainee Department Manager, eventually reaching the status of Department Manager and, ultimately, General Manager. Charles was, himself, a product of this training regime.

The company was subsequently purchased by another company, a Canadian operator which wanted a presence in the UK. This new company had a strong operating philosophy that long-term success was dependent on equal investment in people development and efficiency improvements. In many ways, its operating culture was very different to the one that Charles had presided over and was proud of. The Canadian company had a culture that was based upon the strategic principles developed by Organisational Development researchers Blake and Mouton (1964), who understood that managers had a legitimate concern for production issues. However, they also felt that if managers considered workers in purely economic terms, this would produce an unhealthy mechanical and distorted view of organisational experience. It would inhibit self-actualisation processes, undermine the potential for management and staff collaboration and dilute the motivational capacity of the employee. Such a culture would also constrain organisational learning, discourage leadership and encourage administrative managerial/staff relations. To counter this, Blake and Mouton (1964) argued that what was required was an organisational culture that emphasised to all employees, in equal proportion, the importance of cultivating and continuously developing both the economic and the socio/cultural dimensions of the organisation. This organisational model was called "high performance" and was described as one that invested time in both economic and people-orientated activities.

The Canadian board initiated a staff engagement survey headed up by business researchers throughout their new acquisition and the results overwhelmingly indicated a leadership culture synonymous with anti-conscious leadership.

Sharing the findings

The research team subsequently organised an action research seminar involving Charles and representatives of his senior and middle management team and their equivalents from the new parent company, inclusive of the CEO. The day was to be facilitated by a change management consultant from a prominent local business school. The room was set up with round conference tables, each one accommodating eight people. The managers from Charles's company sat separate from their counterparts from the parent company. This was evidence of the wide differences in operating culture. Charles and his team wore dark suits, white shirts and company ties; the parent company executives wore light coloured suits, soft blue shirts, no ties and kept their suit jackets off, draped over their chairs. Charles and his team were constrained and formal whilst the parent company team was highly animated, laughing and joking and clearly in rapport. The CEO of the parent company then took to the floor and quietly introduced the proceedings, starting off with some light humour. She stated that the aim was to have a healthy discussion about the findings and to look for opportunities for both organisations to start learning how to integrate their beliefs and values to form one new, highly successful organisation.

The day was a disaster. Charles and his team were incredibly defensive. The parent company counterparts were frustrated and confused. This was the coming together of the Greeks and the Spartans. Two completely different leadership cultures. Post-seminar, a decision was taken by the CEO to restructure both organisations and to "colonise" Charles's organisation with leaders modelled in the culture of the parent company. A conscious leadership coaching programme was introduced, a share option scheme for all staff established and an organisation-wide cultural change project was designed and dually implemented. Within 18 months Charles and almost all his management team had left and sought employment in other organisations.

One can see that the company Charles associated with could be described as having a very low concern for people and a very high concern for results. This culture was described by Blake and Mouton (1964) as "Produce-or-Perish Management", whilst the Canadian firm could be described using the framework developed by Blake and Mouton (1964) as "Team Management"; two extreme opposites in terms of business strategies. What follows is an analysis of the above case study adopting a framework which captures key characteristics of anti-conscious leadership.

Disassociated hierarchical culture

The research team documented within the previous case study established that relationships throughout the culture of Charles's company were highly formalised. Management was referred to by their surnames when staff or managers of a lower grade interacted with them. Relationships were characterised by involving dissociated states driven by asymmetrical power relationships. There was little evidence of mutually rewarding social relationships based upon rapport, and the focus of most interactions was either on task achievement or addressing problems identified by management. The flow of communication between management and staff was unilateral, with the senior manager defining the problem and advising the solutions, then delegating responsibilities.

Corrective feedback

Within the case study, organisation staff felt anxious when interacting with line managers. Staff framed these interactions as opportunities for line managers to critique their work, apportion blame and treat them as dependents who needed direction and, thus, told what to do. There was a sense of excessive corrective feedback and a lack of positive feedback. This was very much a leadership culture characterised by management by exception active.

Impoverished leadership style

The case study leadership culture could be described as an impoverished leadership style. In many cases, line managers were benevolent autocrats who minimised the personal development of their direct reports and often adopted body language, tonality and language patterns that were aggressive and demanding whilst signifying a lack of tolerance regarding mistakes and the perspectives of their staff.

Lack of reflexivity

It was noticed from the analysis of the case study that these leadership strategies were employed unreflectively. It did not occur to any of the managers that there was anything irregular or unhelpful regarding their ways of being and interacting with their team members. They all believed that what they were doing was "the way things had always been done around here" and that they were far from being dysfunctional; they were, in fact, behaving in highly proper ways in line with the expectations of the established leadership teams. They did not perceive that they were in any way harming relationships, team working or the potential of the organisational culture to be one that could evolve as a learning organisation. They all came with very positive intentions.

Contingent reward extrinsically orientated

The reward system was very basic, and for all staff, including line management, extrinsic transactions such as career progression at the whim of superiors were the main reward system, although senior management also received performance-related bonuses based upon harsh sales and profit targets. The reward system was extrinsically orientated based on the granting of higher status.

CRASH state and lack of psychological safety

The combined impact of all the above created a culture that could be described as very weak in relation to cohesive and engaged team dynamics. Mistakes were often covered up, a blame culture was normalised, line managers developed highly efficient defensive routines, change was avoided and there was an excessive reliance on traditional problem-solving methods. Staff turnover was high, especially management trainees. There was a lack of transparency and sharing of perspectives throughout the employee culture and an orientation towards compliance and deference to authority. The management culture was in a group CRASH state and dominated by weak psychological safety and as such was:

Contracted: Closed to the ideas and influences of others, self-protective and distrusting.

Reactive: Snapping at situations, responding unreflectively, driven by self-protective and distrusting emotions.

Analysis paralysis: In a state of over-analysing (or over-thinking) a situation.

Separated: Detached from stakeholders and relations, the emphasis being placed on calculative transactional relations and cognitive emotional processes.

Hurt: Involved in feelings of disappointment or rejection towards the wider social field.

Conclusion

The absence of meaningful rapport that is shared throughout the LMX dyads horizontally and vertically to create one composite team of in-group members is a sign of anti-conscious leadership. The lack of rapport is also deemed to be a generator of impoverished personal relations between potential leaders and potential followers. The lack of rapport and the presence of out-groups is a signifier of a lack of leadership reflexivity. Too much or too little corrective feedback contributes towards weak rapport and impoverished personal relations; therefore, leaders need to be skilled at providing constructive feedback that both reinforces excellence and encourages adaptation and learning through personal development. A reliance upon extrinsic rewards and a lack of emphasis on intrinsic rewards leads to a culture that is too task- and production-orientated. The sum effects of all these elements working together can be a lack of psychological safety and a transition towards a group CRASH state that impedes the capacity for organisational learning, especially double loop learning and reflexivity. This corrosive process of anti-conscious leadership will lead the organisation into a state of progressive decline. The role of leadership is to build a culture of reflexivity and positive identification with the organisation's vision, ambition and mission. This involves the establishment of a conscious leadership mindset based upon high levels of emotional intelligence, integral to which is the art and practice of reflexivity, which is the subject of the next chapter when we introduce our blended leadership model.

References

Bowman, S. & Bowman, C. (2014) *Conscious Leadership: The Key to Unlocking Success*. Access Consciousness Publishing Company.

Blake, R. & Mouton, J. (1964) *The Managerial Grid: The Key to Leadership Excellence*. Gulf Publishing Company.

Breukelen, W., Schyns, B. & Blanc, P.M. (2006) Leader-Member Exchange Theory and Research: Accomplishments and Future Challenges. *Leadership*, 2(10).

Dembkowski, S., Eldbridge, F. & Hunter, I. (2006) *The 7 Steps of Effective Executive Coaching*. Thorogood.

Dilts, R. (2003) *From Coach to Awakener*. Meta Publications.

Dilts, R. (2017) *Conscious Leadership and Resilience*. Dilts Strategy Group.

Gallwey, W.T. (1999) *The Inner Game of Work*. Random House Publishing Group.

Graen, G.B. & Uhl-Bien, M. (1995) Relationship-Based Approach to Leadership: Development and Leader-Member Exchange (LMX) Theory of Leadership Over 25 Years: Applying a Multi-Level Multi-Domain Perspective. *Leadership Quarterly*, 6, pp. 219–247.

McCalman, J. & Potter, D. (2015) *Leading Cultural Change: The Theory and Practice of Successful Organizational Transformation*. Kogan Page.

Mead, H.G. (1934) *Mind, Self and Society, from the Stand Point of a Social Behaviourist*. University of Chicago Press.

Northouse, P. (2010) *Leadership Theory and Practice*. Sage.

O'Connor, J. & Seymour, J. (2011) *Introducing NLP: Psychological Skills for Understanding and Influencing People*. HarperCollins.

Omilion-Hodges, L. & Ptacek, J. (2021) *What Is the Leader – Member Exchange (LMX) Theory?* Palgrave Macmillan.

Potter, D. (2018) *Neuro-Linguistic Programming for Change Leaders: The Butterfly Effect*. Routledge.

Schein, H.E. (1985) *Organisational Culture and Leadership*. Jossey-Bass Publishers.

8   A BLENDED MODEL OF LEADERSHIP

Introduction

In this chapter, we introduce our model of "blended leadership" as an alternative leadership framework, which can generate a healthy organisation that has a significant probability of emerging as one that is fit for purpose in the future as well as in the present. Blended leadership can be defined as an integrated model of three leadership styles:

1. Transactional.
2. Transformational.
3. Conscious.

It is our main contention that conscious leadership is the mediator that gives value and practical potential to the emergence and application of effective and high quality transactional and transformational leadership effects. Conscious leadership is to be understood as a way of being internal and external to self (Anderson and Anderson, 2010) to generate high-quality resourceful LMX relationships which enable the emergence of effective transactional and transformational leadership. The emphasis on conscious leadership is placed upon leading one's internal and external states with purpose and awareness inclusive of sensitivity towards the impact we have on others.

A theory of blended leadership

Alvesson et al. (2017) call for a model of leadership that:

1. Is reasonably distinct.
2. Facilitates thinking rather than just sounding good with empty promises.
3. Allows for complexity yet is accessible and encourages critical reflection.

The model of leadership that we advance meets the above criteria. Our model is a blended model that brings together three discreet leadership theories as a

DOI: 10.4324/9781003272793-9

blended model that is both conceptual and inherently practical. Our blended model of leadership also provides the basis for short bursts of learning in workshops for emerging leaders and for a longitudinal leadership development programme (see Figure 8.1).

A meeting of theory with practice

A common fault line that runs through much of the leadership literature is either the over-simplification of the leadership process or the over-complication of it, and, as Alvesson et al. (2017) argue, what we need is a model that sits between simplicity and complexity. We propose a model of blended leadership that meets with this criterion and matches with the reality of leadership efforts within organisations. Therefore, whilst our model of blended leadership has clear conceptual qualities, we will demonstrate in this chapter, and the chapters that follow, its unambiguous practical applications.

Concept review

In previous chapters, we have defined and reviewed transactional and transformational leadership models inclusive of the additive effect as constituted by the sum influence of the Four Is developed by Bass and Avolio (1990a). We have also explained and explored contingent reward as a source of extrinsic motivation and management by exception passive and active as potential disengagement catalysts. Therefore, we shall now explore and review relevant

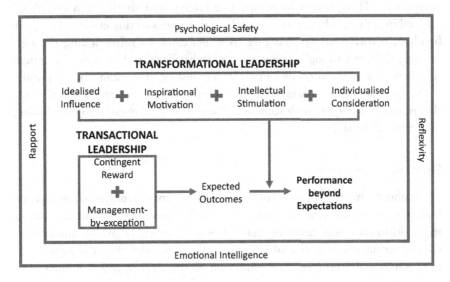

Figure 8.1 Blended Leadership Model

Source: Adapted by Potter and Starke (2020) building upon the Additive Effect Model developed by Bass and Avolio (1990a)

literature regarding the four main elements of our blended leadership model that underpin conscious leadership as one of the three leadership styles that form the blended leadership model. These four elements are:

1. Rapport.
2. Emotional intelligence.
3. Psychological safety.
4. Reflexivity.

Rapport

In Chapter 7, we defined rapport as defined by O'Connor and Seymour (2011, p. 234) as: *"The process of establishing and maintaining a relationship of mutual trust and understanding between two or more people"*. When one is trying to build rapport, one is open to the worldview of the other. The aim is not to internalise the world view of the other; rather, when building rapport, one is aiming to understand and welcome the world view of the other. Rapport is dynamic, fluid and open to change and transformation. Once you are in a state of rapport, you can make efforts to lead the other, and if you apply the techniques of calibrating, matching, eliciting and pacing your audience and engage them in dialogue, you will have an improved chance at leading the shaping of their particular world view. To lead others from a relationship base that is characterised by rapport is far more achievable when the follower is open to appreciating and valuing your point of view. This process involves both the leader and the follower being prepared to be open to considering each other's perspective and potentially integrating these into a new shared perspective. This process of perspective taking, and sharing is a conscious leadership skill. Leading, paradoxically with regards to this model of rapport building, involves subtly changing from matching to mismatching through offering different thought processes and behaviours and inviting the others to follow you. However, one cannot lead unless one has established rapport.

Rapport is both a process of relationship management and a social state, that is, to be in rapport with someone. Rapport is fundamental to establishing conscious leadership.

Emotional intelligence

Throughout Chapter 12, we shall review the concept of emotional intelligence in-depth, so, for now, we shall briefly define it. The concept of intelligence in many organisations is narrowly defined to constituting cognitive capabilities. Clearly, managers as potential leaders need to consider the development of their emotional intelligence as important as the development of their cognitive intelligence. Goleman (2015) argues that cognitive skills are required to master the technical aspects of the function of the executive, though not the social aspect, i.e., how one builds productive leadership/membership exchanges which rely upon enhanced emotional intelligence.

Psychological safety

In Chapter 1, we briefly defined psychological safety as involving feeling safe for interpersonal risk-taking regarding being able to express one's self without fear of any harm to one's self-image, sense of self or career (Kahn, 1990, p. 708). It has also been defined as: "A shared belief that the team is safe for interpersonal risk taking. In psychologically safe teams, team members feel accepted and respected" (Edmondson, 1999). It is understood that when leaders create a field of psychological safety, staff engagement increases significantly. Edmondson (1999, p. 354) explains psychological safety within a group setting as: "A team climate characterized by interpersonal trust and mutual respect in which people are comfortable being themselves". The main characteristics of psychological safety when present in a group are:

1. Interpersonal trust.
2. Mutual respect.
3. Authenticity of self.
4. Group resonance.

Psychological safety is a critical factor, also, in the building of productive teams and a key indicator of the competence of a conscious leader, i.e., the ability to build and nurture a climate of psychological safety in team members (Duhigg, 2016). Psychological safety is also an antecedent and a key factor in enabling the emergence of the model 2 mindset and the establishment of generative dialogue in leadership teams.

Reflexivity and reflection

In Chapter 3, we briefly defined reflexivity, drawing from Alvesson et al. (2017, p. 14), who define reflexivity as: "The ambition to carefully and systematically take a critical view of one's own assumptions, ideas and favoured vocabulary and to consider if alternative ones make sense". Reflexivity is a key leadership competence in the model that we are developing. The distinction between reflection and reflexivity is that reflexivity seeks to explore experience to enable double loop learning, focusing on the utility and foundation of the values and beliefs that drive our perceptions, attitudes and behaviours and, thus, our decisions regarding the organisation and leadership (Argyris and Schön, 1974). The aim of reflexivity, then, is to maintain a flexible approach to our values and beliefs and associated social strategies enabling their maintenance, adaption, deletion or complete transformation. Reflexivity involves a willingness, when required, to adopt different perspectives to move across a continuum from a closed perspective to open, to differentiated, to integrated (Dixon, 1998).

Reflexivity can be considered as a derivative of reflection, and Alvesson et al. (2017) describe the process of reflexivity as "meta-reflection". Meta-reflection is enabled through the process of mindfulness, which can be understood as the ability to pay attention to both internal and external stimuli in the present moment and observe them without judgmental attitudes or cognitive distortions. There have been over 4,000 academic research articles published on mindfulness at work which also signifies a growing corporate interest. Mindfulness allows us to recharge our emotional batteries. It is generally understood that mindfulness enables a healthier body and mind as the mind and the body can be understood as one integrated system. Mindful techniques are also very useful for helping leaders to manage stressful and highly challenging situations. Sometimes as a leader one needs to be fully present and engaged in the moment and practising a mindfulness technique before the situation at hand can elicit such valuable internal resources. The practice of eliciting a shift from CRASH state to COACH state involves mindfulness interventions. In certain organisations it is now standard practice for management teams to start a board room meeting by engaging in a group mindfulness technique to access their COACH states and shake of any CRASH states.

The model of reflexivity that we have briefly surveyed thus far is depicted in Figure 8.2:

Reflexivity, thus, involves a habit of mind that needs to be put into practice daily. Reflexive practice is a key conscious leadership skill set, and it requires a growth mindset and a willingness to explore the premise of our premise and be open to shifting our point of view through dialogue with followers. Reflexivity is a core foundational resource that enables the adoption, expression and sustainability of a model 2 mindset. Finally, it is important to make

Figure 8.2 Reflexivity Process

a distinction between reflexivity and emotional intelligence; the latter focuses on the emotional states we select in response to social situations and the way these emotions of choice generate our behavioural and attitudinal choices. The former is concerned with capturing experiences on action and post-action, as well as future pacing experience pre-action to examine the beliefs and values that are driving our behavioural choices, emotional responses and, thus, generating our social results.

The transactional ingredient of our blend

For something to have a practical value, it needs to be addressing a common problem that is experienced by a critical mass of people. Transactional leadership, we believe, is the fundamental basis of all leadership relationships. It is challenging to conceive of a leadership/followership situation that does not, at its base, have transactions. The contingent reward that underpins the transactional leadership dynamic may be economic, material, emotional, intellectual, ideological or psychological. The reward may be shared between the leader and the follower, or the reward may be different for each party. The main thing is that the contingent reward provides the initial basis for a leadership/followership dynamic to evolve.

The quality of the LMX is the main area that is fraught with possible contamination. It is, as we have discussed previously, entirely possible that the LMX will be one that can be described as an impoverished LMX dynamic. The promised contingent reward may be the only variable that is holding the LMX relationship together. If the leader adopts too crude a transactional strategy, disassociates from their followers, treats them latterly as inanimate objects under the heading of human resources to be used and dispensed with at will and only pays them attention when things go awry, then all of these variables will generate a culture of disengagement with the leader and the work and the organisation at large. This impoverished leadership style will, at best, generate expected outcomes.

The conscious leadership ingredient in our blend

However, when the transactional leadership model is blended with a culture of conscious leadership that privileges human relationships based on principles of strong rapport embedded in a climate of psychological safety, created by leaders who are open to developing their standards of emotional intelligence through reflexive practices, we have the potential of highly enriching LMX developing. This principle opens the proposition that the transactional leadership model is a highly effective model for leading day-to-day operations within an organisation and one that followers can flourish within. There is no reason that a follower may not have their basic, intermediate, and even higher-level motivational level needs met within a transactional leadership culture. This, of course, only occurs if the transactional culture is wrapped in conscious leadership practices supported by a model 2 mindset on the part of the transactional leaders. We see no contradiction in this possibility. However, what we do acknowledge is that such a model requires a curious mind, an openness to learning and introspection and personal development. In other words, a growth mindset.

Transactional leadership has its limitations. It is fine, as stated above, for day-to-day operations and managing and leading staff with conscious awareness through tame and critical problems. However, when it comes to wicked problems, then what is required is an even richer blend of leadership practices and traits. The transaction that binds the leader with the follower needs to be enriched or added to. A wicked problem requires a collaborative approach based on leadership followership dialogue. It also requires a conscious leadership mindset that has powerful transformational tendencies. This leadership moment is when the significance of the quality of the model 2 mindset comes into play. Being open to multiple perspectives, declaring one's assumptions and bias, inviting open enquiry into your perspectives, deeply engaging in reflexive thinking, empathising from a position of curiosity, not judging with stakeholders' perspectives and, finally, being able to hold challenging feelings from a highly resourceful place are all necessary to lead transformational change, i.e., manage a wicked problem with a group of engaged followers.

The transformational ingredient of our blend

Engaging followers in the management of a wicked problem requires transformational leadership supported by a highly enriching transactional base. It also needs the culture of conscious leadership practices to be energised and sustained through habitual modelling of conscious leadership techniques on the part of all highly influential people (Alvesson et al., 2017). Transformational leadership is the term we allocate to a leader who has latterly led a transformation within an organisation.

The concerning theme is that the level of staff disengagement throughout organisations worldwide indicates that transformational change, far from being extraordinary, is, in fact, increasingly becoming ordinary, everyday challenges facing leaders, requiring an extraordinary approach; a blended leadership approach based upon:

- Enriching transactional LMX.
- Model 2 mindset.
- Double loop learning.
- Conscious leadership practices.
- Transformational motivational resources.

We shall explore how to evolve as a conscious leader in the chapters that follow.

The additive effect in our blend

What we do know is that for a transformational change effort to be successful, the leaders need to provide sources of motivation that add to and enrich the basic contingent reward system that sustains the transactional leadership model during normal operational conditions. This requires role models. These role models need to be the change that they want to see in their followers. The additive effect model (see Figure 8.3) provides us with a useful guide to these unique motivational resources that role models should provide followers with if they wish to positively engage them in a transformational change project.

The Four Is

A short case study will illuminate how each of the Four Is can work in practice.

Mr Awarni was a managing director of a substantial engineering firm. He was 50 years of age and a highly experienced executive. His management team were all originally tradespersons who came from a craft background. Mr Awarni realised that he needed a leadership culture that was based on an ability to live both in the present and in the future. His team needed to attend to business, manage in the moment and simultaneously value building strategic competencies that would enable the business to emerge as one that was fit for the future. The enabler of their cultural conversion, he decided, was to provide a learning opportunity based upon personal and group development through an Executive MBA course at a local and highly regarded business school.

He chose not to impose this option on his team; rather, he elected to sign up for the course himself. He intended to lead by example and, thus, provide a source of "idealised influence". Then, he invited his team to a seminar to explore his thoughts regarding the culture he felt was required and offered a compelling vision of the organisation and a clear articulation of his audience's role as leaders in bringing this vision into everyday reality, thus providing a source of "inspirational motivation". This seminar was supported by a graphic illustrator who drew the storyboard of the organisation's past, present and future. He explained his decision to sponsor a corporate MBA programme and

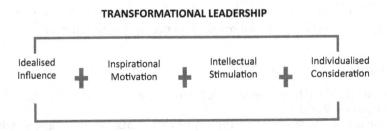

Figure 8.3 The Four Is of Transformational Leadership
Source: Bass and Avolio (1990b)

invited all present to join him on his MBA learning journey, promising all who did full funding and a personal business coach to help guide them through their own personal transformation, thus providing a source of "individualised" consideration.

Finally, the team who attended the MBA journey accessed a rich resource of "intellectual stimulation", working together on applied research projects and working with world-class experts in strategic business functions. After three years, all 15 leaders completed their MBA, and this formed the basis of the organisation's talent management and succession programme; it also led to organisation-wide changes in its branding, operations and customer mix. This example of transformational leadership was supported by all the elements of our blended leadership model.

Conclusion

Our model of blended leadership can be considered as an authentic theory of Praxis, one that has conceptual properties whilst promising practical applications (Gramsci, 1971). Thus our model has two purposes: (1) to offer a model for conceptual learning and understanding of the complexity of leadership that is accessible to all learners; and (2) it offers a model of applied practice that enables leaders to reflect on their own leadership competencies and that of the leadership culture and progress towards a leadership development journey underpinned by practical exercises and learnings. Establishing a shift in leadership/management culture is very much a wicked problem and not a challenge suited to the faint-hearted. It involves emotional, intellectual and cultural resilience. However, it does not need to be a learning experience that is overtly stressful. It can be an enriching and positive learning experience. However, for this to be the case, the leadership must purposefully set out to establish a climate of psychological safety. They must be adept at engaging in dialogue with their followers. They have to be open to personal growth and constructive feedback. And they do need to understand models and frameworks of leadership and cultural change and associated techniques of personal and group development. Thus, they need to demonstrate a healthy growth mindset as well as a highly flexible cognitive intelligence curious about surveying alternative perspectives. All these requirements indicate a need for mature and reflexive emotional and behavioural intelligence. In the next chapter, we shall consider just how a leader would, with conscious awareness, develop conscious leadership potential based upon dialogue with followers.

References

Alvesson, M., Blom, M. & Sveningsson, S. (2017) *Reflexive Leadership: Organising in an Imperfect World.* Sage.

Anderson, D. & Anderson, L. (2010) *Beyond Change Management: How to Achieve Breakthrough Results Through Conscious Change Leadership.* John Wiley and Sons.

Argyris, C. & Schön, D.A. (1974) *Theory in Practice: Increasing Professional Effectiveness.* Jossey-Bass.

Bass, B.M. & Avolio, B.J. (1990a) The Implications of Transactional and Transformational Leadership for Individual, Team, and Organizational Development. *Research in Organizational Change and Development*, 4, pp. 231–272.

Bass, B.M. & Avolio, B.J. (1990b) Developing Transformational Leadership: 1992 and Beyond. *Journal of European Industrial Training*, 14.

Dixon, N.M. (1998) *Dialogue at Work.* Lemos & Crane.

Duhigg, C. (2016) What Google Learned from Its Quest to Build the Perfect Team. *The New York Times Magazine.*

Edmondson, A. (1999) Psychological Safety and Learning Behavior in Work Teams. *Administrative Science Quarterly*, 44(2).

Goleman, D. (2015) *Emotional Intelligence.* Vietnam Labor Publishing House.

Gramsci, A. (1971) *Selections from the Prison Notebooks.* Lawrence and Wishart.

Kahn, W.A. (1990) Psychological Conditions of Personal Engagement and Disengagement at Work. *Academy of Management Journal*, 33, pp. 692–724.

O'Connor, J. & Seymour, J. (2011) *Introducing NLP: Psychological Skills for Understanding and Influencing People.* HarperCollins.

9 THE DIALOGICAL CONSCIOUS LEADER

Introduction

A central aspect of leadership is communication. It has been claimed that communication occupies 70 to 90% of leaders' time every day (Mintzberg, 1973; Eccles et al., 1992). It is also generally understood that good communication and leadership go hand in hand; thus, managers must improve their core communication skills if they are to become effective leaders (Pozin et al., 2017). This developmental requirement is even more fundamental to the prospect of emerging as a conscious leader. Being aware of how we communicate, the effect of our communication methods on followers' states and being able to select specific modes of communication with awareness and purpose are critical conscious leadership competencies. Improving upon our communication skills with both awareness and purpose is a continuous process. In this chapter, we define leadership communication. We then explore in detail the concept of the dialogically conscious leader as a central feature of the conscious leader's identity and skill set. We emphasise dialogue because this is the main mode of communication that differentiates conscious leaders from managers and from transactional leaders.

Defining leadership communication

Unfortunately, many leaders have their potential underdeveloped as they are in a state of unconscious incompetence when it comes to the range of communication methods open to them and how, in practice, to adopt enriching communications. Barret (2006, p. 1) claims that: "The sheer amount of time managers spend communicating underscores how important strong communication skills can be for the manager desiring to advance to leadership positions; thus, mastering leadership communication should be a priority for managers wanting their organizations or the broader business community to consider them leaders". To lead with conscious awareness requires sensitivity towards both the quality of one's communications and the model of communication being adopted. Communication has been thoughtfully defined by Luthra (2015, p. 3.) as follows: "Leadership communication is defined as inspiring and encouraging an individual or a group by systematic and

DOI: 10.4324/9781003272793-10

meaningful sharing of information by using excellent communication skills".
By quality, we refer to the clarity, relevant content, engagement impact, and
the outcome of shared understanding and agreement to act or not to act.

Conscious leaders are, by our definition, meaning-makers; they facilitate
sense-making internal and external to self and do this mainly through communication and, of course, modelling the behaviours and standards they are asking for in others. Leadership communication is also defined by Barret (2006,
p. 5) as follows: "Leadership communication is the controlled, purposeful
transfer of meaning by which leaders influence a single person, a group, an
organization, or a community. Leadership communication uses the full range
of communication skills and resources to overcome interferences and to create
and deliver messages that guide, direct, motivate, or inspire others to action".
Barret (2006, p. 5) places central to her definition of leadership communication the "purposeful transfer of meaning by which leaders influence a single
person, a group, an organisation, or a community". This supports our understanding of conscious leadership as the meaning that is created or intended is
meaning communicated thoughtfully and with acute awareness. This definition is in keeping with the Alvesson and Sveningsson (2008) conception of
leaders as "meaning-makers".

Conscious leadership communication involves the considerate crafting of
message content and style of delivery inclusive of tonality and physical expression. Conscious leadership communication also involves adopting an empathetic position in relation to one's intended audience and imagining the effect
the communication will have on their state, future pacing the delivery of the
message and refining it. Future pacing basically involves "Mentally rehearsing
an outcome to ensure that the desired behaviour will occur" (O'Connor and
Seymour, 2011, p. 231).

Dialogue

Dialogue is a form of developmental communication that is the key to
unlocking the developmental potential of both the individual and the group.
Specifically, dialogue is defined by Isaacs (1999, p. 9) as: "A shared enquiry,
a way of thinking and reflecting together". Dialogue aims to achieve a state
of shared meaning between participants. We define dialogue as: "The art of
thinking together with conscious awareness using our cognitive mind and
somatic system". We include the somatic system to address the way in which
feelings inform our behavioural expressions as well as our cognitive mind,
which informs our thinking strategies. As conscious leaders, we acknowledge
that the way in which we interpret the meanings of things is based upon
both our somatic and cognitive responses. For example, when arriving at
an important decision, we may consider several differentiated perspectives.
Our somatic (physical and emotional) internal response to each perspective
will have to be congruent with our cognitive response. Thus, we may be
presented with five different solutions based on the unique perspective of

a group of team members and, emotionally and physically, three out of five might unsettle our somatic state and make us feel uncomfortable, and so, cognitively, we reject these. The remaining two might feel comfortable, and so, emotionally, we are curious to explore the finer details of these two possible choices.

When engaging in dialogue with conscious awareness, the conscious leader would explain to the team the problem that they have. Then they would describe how they are "feeling" in relation to this problem. They would describe the beliefs and values that underpin their interpretation of the significance of the problem. Then they would invite each team member to reflect on the problem and offer a reframing of the content and/or context of the problem as described from the team leader's perspective. As each team member offers a reframe, the leader would listen with curiosity and internally assess their feelings and emotions and their physicality, i.e., their body posture. Behavioural change expert Robert Dilts advocates accessing one's inner coach to meta reflect on how one is managing one's emotions resourcefully. For example, as the leaders go through this inner dialogue when they feel themselves moving towards a CRASH state in response to a perspective being offered, or even perspectives, they would ask themselves:

How am I feeling just now?

And then, after they get an internal response, they would ask:

How do I feel about feeling that way?
How is the way I am feeling influencing the way I am thinking about these perspectives?
How are my physical states, emotional states and thinking states affecting how I am being received by my audience?

And then:

Is there another state that I could access that would help me and my team be more open to these perspectives?
Inspiration from the work of Robert Dilts – www.nlpu.com

Then the leader recalls an experience when they were able to listen to challenging perspectives with curiosity and patience, and they, in that moment, fully associate with that experience and the feelings, bodily posture and thoughts and, perhaps, make a private somatic gesture such as nodding of the head to intensify their desire to be open, curious and patient.

Internally focused dialogue involves internal calibration and reflection and the ability to identify one's states and engage with your "inner coach" to win the inner game in that moment (Gallwey, 1999). The concept of the inner coach is based on the principle that we can create internal identity parts using our conscious mind, for example, "sporty me", "sociable me" or "competitive me". These parts of our identity reside deep within our unconscious mind and present themselves when situations expect them or need them to turn up. As conscious leaders, we can create other support members of our cast of internal identity parts such as "me the carer", "me the learner" or "me the coach to me". The latter identity part is our internal coach. Our internal coach is the identity part that we would use to facilitate an internal dialogue. Our internal coach is our creation and acts purely with positive intentions to serve us and enable our personal development. However, it needs coaching tools, and so the "I" of us has a responsibility to study and learn and practice our learnings as conscious leaders so that we can feed our inner coach with the capabilities it needs to serve us in our personal journey of growth and self-discovery. To be a conscious leader from a dialogical perspective means being prepared to:

1. Acknowledge one's closed perspective and the defensive routines protecting it.
2. To actively and with awareness seek rapport both internal and external to self.
3. Be open to exploring alternative perspectives from a position of internal dialogue.
4. Be able to access and develop one's inner coach to enable this process of perspective-taking.
5. Be open to identifying the differentiated nature of different perspectives from a place of curiosity and patience.
6. Have the willingness and skills to pace the perspectives of others and engage them in a process of dialogue.
7. Create a field of psychological safety through which the group can engage in a dialogue and welcome each other's unique perspectives and, again, be open to appreciating differentiated perspectives.
8. Move the collective intelligence of the group to let go of closed perspectives and to agree to co-author a new integrated perspective as a basis of collective action owned by the group.

Investing in dialogue

Nancy Dixon (1998) makes the very practical point that to engage in an ongoing dialogue those participating in a dialogue session would need space and time for doing so. However, to allocate the time required and introduce the enabling vehicles, the dialogue process must be valued by organisational leaders and their teams. This means that the organisation must explore what its members believe to be true regarding such an investment in time and energy. This awakening process is an act of conscious leadership. The main challenge we feel with the idea of engaging in a systematic programme of dialogue is that it is a practice that is likely to be understood by only a small number of people with specialised knowledge or interest.

Dixon (1998) also points out that in many business schools throughout the world, the emphasis is on instrumental learning and not communicative learning, the latter being underpinned by dialogue and the former by alternative modes of communication such as discussion or monologue. The skills and knowledge required regarding the functionality of managing an organisation fall within instrumental learning, whilst the process of running dialogue seminars falls within communicative learning. Dixon (1998, p. 35), referring to the work of Jack Mezirow (1991), defines instrumental learning as: "Learning that leads to the control and manipulation of the environment, which in this definition includes other people". In contrast, she defines communicative learning as involving the task of: "Learning to understand what others mean and to make oneself understood. The goal of communicative learning is to gain insight and to reach common understanding rather than to control". Communicative learning is supported by emancipatory learning when engaging in a dialogue.

The goal of emancipatory learning is described by Dixon (1998, p. 37), again drawing inspiration from Mezirow (1991), as: "To identify and reflect on distorted meaning perspectives". Human beings socially construct their reality perspectives, and these constructions emerge as frames through which they make sense of the world. The function of dialogue is to reveal the distorted realities that hold people back from crafting the kind of culture that enables high-level individual and group development.

As dialogue is not established as a normative and familiar organisational practice, the only way to embed it as a valued practice supported by enabling beliefs regarding its value is to simply organise a dialogue about doing dialogue. This is to create an internal market for the establishment and provision of organised dialogue sessions. If the participants enjoy the initial dialogue and conclude that they appreciate its worth, then they may, through free will, choose to continue with the practice and slowly establish dialogue as the cultural norm throughout the organisation at large.

Dialogue and conscious leadership awakening

Isaacs (1999, p. 3) states that: "How we think does affect how we talk and how we talk together definitively determines our effectiveness . . . the problems that even the most practical organizations have in improving their performance and obtaining the results they desire can be traced directly to their inability to think and talk together, particularly at critical moments". Conscious leadership involves a sensitivity and appreciation of the forms of talk that define and limit the scope and range of perspective-taking and organisational learning. We already know that management teams establish linguistic-based defensive routines which insulate the model 1 mindset and an anti-conscious leadership culture from change. These are cultural norms of communicating and sense-making that maintain and advance their own operating culture. We also know that corporate hegemony is dependent on its survival and prosperity upon habitual everyday forms of talk (McCalman and Potter, 2015).

As a conscious leader, to change the culture of your team, you need to work through a process of awakening regarding the language that generates and supports "the architecture of the invisible" (Isaacs, 1999, p. 3); the forms of talk that maintain the status quo. Conscious leaders need to develop a form of conscious enquiry into the cultural forces within their corporate culture that often operate below the surface of everyday conversations. These deeply rooted cultural norms tend to block conversation and subsequent group and individual learning. Language is the main sense making enabler that sustains the potency of expressive hegemony to ensure that established culture flourishes. Conscious leaders aim to make their leadership teams aware of these barriers to conscious leadership cultural change work, and they achieve this goal through generative dialogue. We include the word generative to emphasise the premise that change is the desired outcome of the dialogue.

Dialogue, the key to conscious leadership awakening

Dialogue is enabled through social interaction, and particpants have to agree by their own free agency to engage in "a shared enquiry, a way of thinking and reflecting together" (Isaacs, 1999, p. 3). It is the role of the conscious leaders in organisations to build the capacity for dialogical exchange within their community of followers. There are two main types of dialogue: (1) generative, which involves a leader generating dialogical exchanges across an organisation; and (2) reflective, which is a form of private dialogue with the self.

Chris Argyris (1990) considered dialogue as the means to transforming a leadership team's potential for learning. This idea is now established as "the learning organisation" (Senge, 1990). Dialogue has the potential for enabling the establishment of a conscious leadership culture. It can generate new cultural understandings and new ways of expressing oneself within society. Thus, at its heart, dialogue is integral to demonstrating and maintaining a healthy model 2 leadership mindset at the level of the individual and of the group. The acid test of the ability of conscious leaders to flourish and support cultural change efforts is whether dialogue sessions can occur and whether the management team can:

- Discuss the dialogical process together.
- Agree to participate in such a process.
- Fully support the outcome of dialogical encounters.

Dialogue aims to surface all points of view and then encourage open consideration to create a dialectic tension that enables a new perspective to emerge, rooted in the collective view. Thus, the ability to engage in both reflective and generative dialogue is central to the operation of a model 2 mindset and the development of a conscious leadership culture. Dialogue can work to bring teams from different cultures together. The process of cultural change in organisations which essentially involves changing core beliefs and values can be and is enabled through dialogue exchanges between participants. Dialogue does this as it encourages empathy.

The process of collaborating and thinking through the nature of a change problem is enabled through the conscious leader encouraging dialogue. The tendency to engage in monologue expressed through a model 1 mindset does inhibit the accessing of the collective intelligence of the group. Dialogue mediates new shared frames of social reality and, therefore, is fundamental to leadership. Dialogue is central to the effectiveness of the conscious leadership awakening process.

The quality of the dialogue does depend on the use of appropriate techniques and the nature of our relationships with those we are to dialogue with. Often, if a participant is reluctant to transition from a model 1 to a model 2 mindset to engage in a dialogue with others, it is because they do not value the perspective of the other and/or they feel that the dialogue threatens their status in relation to the other participants. This is the time when defensive routines can manifest, and they may be presented as complaints that the talk is unnecessary, time-consuming and not practically connected to "real time" operational issues.

Whilst it is important to acknowledge these defensive routines in terms of the positive intention behind them for the individual, they must be managed productively to reconnect with the dialogue process. This involves establishing within the dialogue seminar equality of voice and a climate of supporting psychological safety. Therefore, the difference between communicative learning and instrumental learning needs to be shared with participants. Instrumental learning involves the subject-object relationship, e.g., "I-It" or "Me and the Other" relationships, which tend to be disassociated and maintained through power distance. In contrast, communicative learning involves person-to-person relationships; "I and Thou".

Martin Buber developed his concept of *"I and Thou"* (Ich und Du, 1923), which is very relevant to understanding the distinction between instrumental and communicative learning. Buber advanced a philosophy asserting the premise that human relationships may be understood by the way in which we engage in dialogue with each other. According to Buber, human beings may adopt two contrasting social strategies when interacting with others which can be understood as either *"I-Thou"* or *"I-It"*.

I-Thou is a relation of person-to-person. In contrast, *I-It* is a relation of person-to-object. The former is based upon an associated communicative and human-centric approach to relationships, whilst the latter is based upon a disassociated instrumental relationship which objectifies the other person or persons in the relationship. If we reconnect with the definition of dialogue as "the art of thinking together" (Isaacs, 1999), *I-Thou* is a relation in which *I* and *Thou* have a shared reality based on dialogue. In contrast, the *I-It* relationship has limited, if any, shared reality; therefore, a dialogue between actors is highly unlikely. As a result of lack of dialogue, the *I* which exists without a relational *Thou* has a weaker perceptual map that is less complete than that of the *I* in the *I-Thou*, which, due to dialogue, share a richer perceptual map and, thus, have greater behavioural flexibility. The more that *I* and *Thou* share their reality, the more complete their reality. Dixon (1998) makes the point that instrumental learning is embedded in the term human resource management (HRM) as HRM signifies an instrumental and objectified relationship between staff who are resources to be controlled and manipulated by managers. This is the "I-It" relationship personified. Conscious leadership enabled through dialogue seminars aims to reframe the "I-It" relationship dynamic to the communicative alternative of "I-Thou".

Conclusion

In conclusion, the capacity for dialogue is dependent on fluid and open social interaction supported by a climate of psychological safety. Defensive routines and inhibiting loops may block or disrupt fluid interaction and expression, which is defined as a group being able to both welcome and encourage the free, uninhibited thinking and expression of others. A major blockage in an organisation could be the status of one person, or group, in relation to others in the organisation. Status confers knowledge and speech rights. These cultural norms, if they are possessively guarded, are effectively major impediments to dialogical exchange. They need to be suspended if dialogue is to be accomplished and future generative dialogue is to take place, i.e., dialogue that generates change. Clearly, this is an incredibly sensitive change process. Dialogue is not necessarily always a rational process as it puts our thoughts, values and assumptions out there for open review. This makes the dialogue process a highly delicate affair. How we "feel" deeply impacts what we think and how we feel about others will also impact us at an emotional level when we go public with our inner thoughts, values and assumptions. Leaders in organisations also have an inner ecology of thoughts, experiences, ideas, assumptions, values and feelings that guide actions which they guard very intensely. Being able to welcome others' perspectives and comments on our own perspectives is an act of conscious leadership. In the next chapter, we shall look at the structure of an applied dialogue seminar from a highly practical perspective.

References

Alvesson, M. & Sveningsson, S. (2008) *Changing Organizational Culture: Cultural Change Work in Progress*. Routledge.

Argyris, C. (1990) *Overcoming Organizational Defenses*. Prentice-Hall.

Barret, F.L. (2006) Are Emotions Natural Kinds? *Sage Journals*, 1(1).

Buber, M. (1923) *Ich und Du*. Im Insel-Verlag zu Leipzig.

Dixon, N.M. (1998) *Dialogue at Work*. Lemos & Crane.

Eccles, R.G., Nohria, N. & Berkley, J.D. (1992) *Beyond the Hype: Rediscovering the Essence of Management*. Harvard Business School Press.

Gallwey, W.T. (1999) *The Inner Game of Work*. Random House Publishing Group.

Isaacs, W. (1999) *Dialogue and the Art of Thinking Together*. Double Day.

Luthra, A. (2015) Effective Leadership Is All About Communicating Effectively. *Connecting Leadership and Communication*, 5(3), pp. 43–48.

McCalman, J. & Potter, D. (2015) *Leading Cultural Change: The Theory and Practice of Successful Organizational Transformation*. Kogan Page.

Mezirow, J. (1991) *Transformative Dimensions of Adult Learning*. Jossey-Bass.

Mintzberg, H. (1973) *The Nature of Managerial Work*. Harper & Row.

O'Connor, J. & Seymour, J. (2011) *Introducing NLP: Psychological Skills for Understanding and Influencing People*. HarperCollins.

Pozin, M.A.A., Nawi, M.N.M., Azman, M.N.A. & Lee, A. (2017) Improving Communication in Managing Industrialised Building System (IBS) Projects: Virtual Environment. *Malaysian Construction Research Journal*, 2(Special Issue 2), pp. 1–13.

Senge, P. (1990) *The Fifth Discipline: The Art and Practice of the Learning Organization*. Doubleday/Currency.

10 PREPARING FOR AND ACTIONING A DIALOGUE SEMINAR

Introduction

Having both reviewed the literature on dialogue and practised dialogue, drawing on the ideas of Nancy Dixon (1998), we have created a framework for establishing a dialogue seminar. To expand upon the practical value of our framework, we shall introduce an action research strategy as an awakening device in advance of a dialogue seminar. This chapter will explore a range of dialogical techniques that a conscious leader may engage with to start facilitating the learning of conscious leadership capabilities on the part of both themselves and team members. The emphasis is placed upon dialogue because, as a special kind of talk, dialogue involves diverse perspective-taking and increasing one's levels of self-awareness through quality relationships.

Stage 1: gather data

The client would ideally appoint an internal or external consultant to lead an action research initiative. The consultant operating as a researcher would employ the following research methods to gather data regarding the change problem:

1. One-to-one, semi-structured interviews with line managers.
2. Focus groups with extended groups of managers and team members.
3. Survey targeting a larger sample of staff members.

This approach would allow for the triangulation of data findings to identify patterns across all three samples. This helps to address issues of validity which means that the data findings are reliable, considering other variables. The mixed research strategy would involve conducting a stakeholder engagement health check audit. Ideally, in excess of 25% of the overall staff population would be surveyed, and the sample would match the staff demographic

DOI: 10.4324/9781003272793-11

profile. The research strategy would be called an "engagement audit" and would aim to research the following stakeholder engagement dimensions:

- Role engagement.
- Vision engagement.
- Mission engagement.
- Leadership engagement.
- Peer group engagement.
- Inter-peer group engagement.
- Task engagement.
- Personal development engagement.

The proposition underpinning such a research project would be that staff disengagement can be driven by anti-conscious leadership culture, and staff engagement by conscious leadership cultures. Therefore, by evaluating the strengths of each staff engagement variable, this can provide a set of performance indicators that can be further investigated to establish their causes in relation to their status. For example, if engagement with personal development is very weak, the research team would want to know why this is the case. The same would be for leadership engagement on the part of followers. Thus, disengagement is a symptom of an underlying problem as opposed to being the problem in itself.

Stage 2: analyse and interpret data findings

The data, once gathered, would then be analysed. One-to-one interviews would be recorded and transcribed, and recurring themes coded. Focus groups would capture their findings on flipchart sheets and post-it notes which, again, would be organised around recurring themes and coded as with the interviews. The survey would be sent out electronically, and, again, the findings would be analysed for patterns. The researcher would then look to triangulate (identify patterns across the three data sets) the findings across all three methods. The results would then be analysed and organised, and a feedback report presented to the executive team. From the analysis of the findings, the researcher could suggest, if findings indicated, probable areas of staff disengagement such as:

- Role engagement.
- Organisational vision.
- Organisational mission.
- Line management relationships.
- Task engagement.

And they would balance this with suggested examples of staff engagement if the data indicated these, for example:

- Departmental peer group engagement.
- Inter-peer group engagement.
- Personal development engagement.

It is important that the data generated by the staff survey, the one-to-one leadership interviews and the focus groups support the findings from the survey report.

Stage 3: create a report of key findings and implications

Following detailed analysis of the returned data sets the consultant researcher would then compose a report that discusses the main themes that were identified from the research process. This report should be written in a way that is accessible to the client community.

Stage 4: share report with the client for evaluation

The consultant researcher would share the report directly with the management team through an action learning workshop. The aim would be to reach consensus regards the implications of the report and agree of a plan of future actions based upon its content. This consensus building process must be handled sensitively to avoid any possible conflict.

Stage 5: agree on action

The management team, in conjunction with the researcher, would agree on a course of future actions based on their sense-making of the research findings report. The consultant may, at this stage, also suggest that the client should establish a series of dialogue seminars to explore the possible drivers based on respondents' lived experience which generated the levels of disengagement and engagement. Therefore, they could propose an initial two-day pilot dialogue seminar to test the commitment of key participants to support such an approach and the organisation's cultural readiness for the practices associated with dialogue. The pilot scheme is a productive strategy to flush out defensive barriers that have built up over time to collaboration, shared sense-making and conscious leadership practices.

The consultants could suggest, as a final recommendation, that such an exercise could start the process of transitioning from a culture based upon transactional leadership models that are often impoverished to a leadership culture synonymous with an enriching blended conscious leadership model. The strategy below details some recommendations for delivering the dialogue seminars.

Dialogue seminars

A key question is, "how many participants should be involved in a dialogue seminar?" The answer, from the perspective of Dixon (1998), is up to 20 participants to enable a productive dialogue. If there are up to 80 potential participants, then the strategy would simply involve multiple dialogue streams. The seminar should last for as long as it takes to explore the themes of the dialogue, as participants will intuitively know when they have reached a conclusion that works for the group. However, managers like to know how long the dialogue will last, and it is suggested that an initial dialogue would be for two days; thereafter, every eight weeks, the team would come together for ongoing dialogue seminars. In our experience, it is more productive to have short, intense dialogue sessions lasting no longer than 1–2 days which yield productive and meaningful results for all participants. Thereafter, we would use this positive experience as a launching pad for the next dialogue seminar in eight weeks' time. This process of incremental dialogue steps provides the opportunity of embedding the dialogue seminars into the cultural fabric of the organisation.

Psychogeography

Robert Dilts (2003, p. 9) states that: "Psychogeography refers to the influence that micro geographical arrangements and relationships exert on people's psychological processes and interpersonal interactions". Thus, if you want to build rapport between participants in a dialogue seminar, then how you arrange the room is very important. Establishing a sense of psychological safety is a critical aspect of a successful dialogue seminar. For example Dixon (1998) advocates the use of circles to emphasise equality of active participants and encourage open and authentic sharing of perspectives. It is often a point missed by managers when organising dialogue sessions or workshops with regard to the impact that furniture arrangements have on social interactions. How you arrange the room for a dialogue really does matter regarding encouraging a willingness to contribute openly on the part of participants.

If a conscious leader brings an audience together for a dialogue seminar in a classroom-style format, using PowerPoint as the main medium, this is fine if all you want is to deliver a personal monologue; however, it may disable dialogue, and it is unlikely that your audience will feel psychologically safe to indulge in dialogue together. So, think through issues such as:

- Ventilation.
- Music.
- Lighting.
- Seating.
- Space to work in pairs and teams.
- Catering.
- Spatial configuration.

These all influence the quality of the dialogue that is going to manifest in your audience.

The importance of investing resources into preparing for the dialogue

Managers are used to thinking in instrumental terms. They are programmed to think of cost and to practise prudent cost management behaviours. They normally have responsibilities for teams and the operating budgets for these teams. It is important that this dynamic is attended to if the idea is to move towards a conscious leadership culture built around dialogue seminars. If, for example, 20 managers are invited to attend a two-day dialogue seminar, then they may be wondering what the practical value of this cost is in terms of "opportunity cost", i.e., the net cost of the time of 20 managers over two days and how this resource could have been used. It is quite understandable to imagine that the idea of attending "extended talking shops" would be a concern to many a pragmatic manager with limited, if any, experience of working with conscious leadership methods and understanding of their mid- to long-term value to a business. Therefore, how we frame the dialogue seminar is critical to securing their support and willingness to continue committing their own and their team members' time to ongoing dialogue seminars.

Initial framing

Ideally, each participant should receive a letter or email inviting them to meet with the Head of Department or a senior Director for coffee to discuss the idea of the dialogue seminar and to explain its importance as a strategic change initiative. This event would ideally be held in a high-status venue such as a board room. The invitation should provide a brief outline of the intention to pilot dialogue seminars and what their purpose is with regard to understanding how best to build higher levels of staff engagement throughout the business. The letter of invite should also explain the importance of the invitees' role in this process. The host, as the significant executive, would pace the experience and mindset of the invitees, acknowledging their potential concerns and assuring them that this is not a whimsical talking shop; rather, it is a serious opportunity for managers to share their ideas, thoughts and concerns in a positive dialogue that will inform the ongoing strategic change initiatives of the business.

The first day

When the managers attend the initial dialogue seminar, the aim of the first day is to totally immerse the participants in a series of dialogical exercises and introduce them, implicitly, through role play to key conscious leadership tools and frameworks. In keeping with the spirit and operating philosophy of the seminal work on strategic behavioural change and intervention (Argyris, 1971), the aim of day one is to build a platform of free will on the part of the managers to continue the dialogue seminars beyond the initial pilot scheme. Argyris recognises that unless managers elect by free will to invest their identity, emotions, time and intellect in a change project, then the likelihood of success will be impaired. To build their commitment, Argyris (1971) asserted that they must have access to valid data and experience change techniques first-hand if they are to arrive at an informed decision regarding their commitment levels. Therefore, day one of the two-day pilot dialogue seminar should explore the utility of the dialogue seminar as a change management tool to generate valid data and create an opportunity for managers to exercise free will in relation to their support or rejection of the approach.

A useful strategy to enable the generation of valid data and the expression of free will on the part of participants is to invite each of them to prepare a personal statement exploring the following question: "*What value do you place on participating in this seminar and why?*" Participants would then prepare and bring a 250-word statement that sets out their personal perspective regarding this question with them to the seminar.

The ten-minute open frame

Dialogue seminars should not have PowerPoint slides, lecterns or tables. These objects are anchors that connect people to the emotional states they associate with meetings and seniority in specific team members. The seminar should be facilitated rather than led or controlled. The facilitator should not be a member of the senior team; rather, a skilled facilitator ideally trained in the facilitation of dialogue seminars. The seminar should be punctuated with ten-minute open frames enabled by the dialogue facilitator. The idea behind an open frame is to frame each segment of the dialogue seminar for participants, and this involves a short briefing together with the opportunity for participants to ask questions and share their thoughts regarding the process.

The senior management present should not adopt their official capacity in any way as they are participants. The initial open frame should:

1. Introduce the aim of the dialogue seminar, inclusive of an explanation of what dialogue involves and the code of conduct that participants should respect when involved in the dialogue seminar.
2. Include a briefing on the concept of perspective-taking.

It is important to start the interactions between participants at the very beginning of the seminar and not allow them to get into an observer state by being exposed to too lengthy a monologue by the facilitator at the start of the day. Thus, this is another key feature of a dialogue seminar; it is not a classroom; rather, it is a space where people interact and think together through the sharing of experiences and the active process of perspective transitioning. The purpose of the ten-minute open frame event is to punctuate this process, allow a mental break from the dialogue and allow each group to connect with the total group system in the room and to have a perceptual map through which they may navigate the seminar.

Perspective transitioning stage 1

After the initial open frame, the facilitator organises participants into groups of three and asks each one to share an account of their unique perspective regarding the value they feel they place on dialogue seminars, uninterrupted, with the group. No time limits should be set to complete this process. It is important that the other two participants do not comment on the perspective statement; rather, they are to ask some questions to help them learn more about the logic behind the individual's perspective. Each of the three participants will have an equal opportunity to share their unique perspective. The point of this reflective and interactive exercise is as an ice breaker and a way to start the dialogue process.

Nancy Dixon (1998) advances the idea that dialogue is essentially involved in exploring alternative perspectives (see Figure 10.1), which involves a process of awakening for participants.

As conscious leaders, we aim to reflect upon our initial perspective towards a social object and, so, raise our conscious awareness regarding the beliefs and values that underpin its form. This initial stage of perspective awakening, as illuminated in the previous exercise, involves reflecting on our closed perspective, which is our perspective that, up to the point of reflective awakening, was closed to alternative interpretations and operated beneath conscious

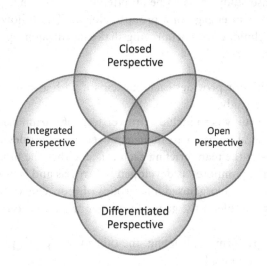

Figure 10.1 Four Strategies for Perspective Taking

Source: Adapted from Dixon (1998)

awareness. The exercise of composing perspective statements triggers the reflective awakening process and reveals the nature of our closed perspective.

Sharing our perspective with others and then listening to other perspectives on the subject helps us move from a closed to an open perspective. The reflective question element of this exercise aids this awakening and transitioning process. Having "transitioned" to an open perspective, we can still own our initial perspective, although we are now opened to acknowledging the rights of others to hold their own perspective, which may be similar, or very different, to our own. The aim of dialogue seminars is to enable this transition from closed to open perspectives.

Sharing our model of the world with others and then graduating to adopting a differentiated perspective which involves acknowledging shades of difference between our initial perspective and those of others, enriches our perceptual maps.

The dialogue, as it progresses, aims to move the participants to a higher level of thinking together. This process enables the co-authorship of a group-integrated perspective that is shared by the group. This will allow participants to let go of their initial perspective as they will have reframed their initial perspective through dialogue with colleagues.

With this exercise, all participants will have practised acknowledging their closed perspective and being open to learning about other perspectives, thus transitioning to an open perspective. It is important to acknowledge that, often, participants are in a state of unconscious competence when it comes to perspective-taking.

The case study approach

The use of a case study can also be an effective way to engage with participants and help them engage in a group dialogue. The following exercise is a productive technique for encouraging dialogue through open perspective-taking in teams.

1. The facilitator provides each participant with a short handout detailing a case study.
2. The case study is to include two versions of a team briefing delivered by a general manager to their team regarding a sales issue. The two versions of the team briefing each reflect either the model 1 or model 2 leadership mindset as developed by Argyris and Schön (1974).
3. Participants are organised into groups of four. One of the participants acts out the role of the general manager and enacts one version of the briefing.
4. As they perform the briefing, the other three participants act out the role of team members.
5. Then, without any comment from the participants, another team member acts out the role of the General Manager and role-plays the performance of the second version of the team briefing.

6. And then, having listened to the story, each member imagines that they were part of the experience the story is based upon and describe to each other how they feel in relation to:

- Asking questions.
- Commenting on what was said.
- Offering suggestions.
- Supporting the initiative.
- Key relationships.

The story

First version

Fiona is a middle manager responsible for the accounts department in a busy city centre hotel. She is invited to attend an emergency management team meeting and represent her department. There are nine other managers present, including the hotel's General Manager, called Alex. The meeting is held in one of the hotel's executive meeting rooms around a large oval mahogany board room table. Each manager arrives slightly early, and they help themselves to tea and coffee and take a seat. Alex arrives last, hastily grabs a coffee and sits at the head of the table. He mumbles a brief "good afternoon" and then places his notes in front of him and passes around an agenda for the meeting. He clears his throat and starts talking:

> As you all know, the economic climate is tough, and it is getting tougher. Customers are increasingly looking for added value, and for them, that usually means they want the cheapest price they can squeeze out of us. It is becoming increasingly clear that sales are not as they should be, and we need to protect the bottom line. We all know that it's time to tighten our belts and make some difficult financial cutbacks to make sure we arrive on budget this year. So I am sure it will make sense to all of you that we need a 10% saving from all departments on their expenditure lines. This is what our industry competitors are all doing, and it's so important we do not get left behind. Now, it's also important that you all support this plan, and that is why I have asked you all to come in today. I want you all to feel that you have been consulted as your support is very important to me. Now, I am sure that you don't want me to waste your valuable time any more than I need to though any questions would be welcomed.
>
> (Alex looks at his watch).

Second version

> Thank you for all coming in this afternoon . . . I appreciate that your time is valuable, so thank you. (Alex looks at each participant as he speaks. Alex then carefully takes off his jacket and loosens his tie.) I realise that

we are all very proud of the service we provide all our customers, and thank goodness I have a team with that mindset as the trading position is growing increasingly challenging. Our consumers do have increased choice out there and are increasingly looking for added value deals. This dynamic is affecting our sales and, unfortunately, we are looking at a significant sales decline. Our board is getting nervous and is pressurising us to make savings to protect shareholder value. I must admit that I do have some sympathy with that proposition, though I am concerned that it could also be a knee jerk reaction that may not sit comfortably with our trading philosophy as a team, which has always looked to put quality first. It is important that you can explore with me the way I am thinking at present, as this issue will and does affect us all. So I thought we could all discuss this situation and allow each of us to share our own perspectives and ideas of how best to respond to the situation, as I would prefer a team-based solution to our problem. So who feels like they would like to start off our discussion?

7. The facilitator then invites participants to share with the wider group their reflections regarding the role play situation and how they feel in relation to both versions of the team briefing. The facilitator then explains that version one of the team briefing is an example of Argyris and Schön's (1974) Model 1 leadership mindset and points out how, in the text, the Hotel Manager:

   • Framed the problem in such a way as to get the other person to agree with one's own view.
   • Advocates their own view in a manner that limits others' questioning of it.

   Then they would illustrate the aspects of version two of the team briefing which is related to Chris Argyris's Model 2 leadership mindset and points out how, in the text, the Hotel Manager advocates their own view and reasoning in a way that encourages others to confront it and to help the speaker discover where the view might be mistaken.

8. This concludes with the facilitator asking participants to take ten minutes, in different groups of four, to discuss which model they would prefer to use or experience as leaders and as members of a leadership team. This exercise is designed to implicitly teach some of the key ideas of Chris Argyris that we feel are highly relevant to emerging as a conscious leader.

Once this dialogue session is complete, the facilitator highlights, for the group, some key principles of dialogue in terms of best practice. The facilitator sets the scene for this stage of the dialogue seminar by exploring with the group the fundamental question, *"Is dialogue about technique or relationship, or both?"* The answer to this question is that dialogue involves a fine balance between applied techniques and the nature of our relationships with others.

Closing stage of the dialogue seminar

The final stage of the dialogue seminar involves participants reflecting together on the possible drivers of staff disengagement and engagement highlighted in the staff survey findings report. This final stage connects the actual process of dialogue with communicative learning. The technique to enable this final dialogue is as follows:

1. Participants are allocated into different groups of four.
2. Participants are given sticky note post-its.
3. There are two colours: green and yellow.
4. Participants write down on green post-its possible reasons for staff disengagement relative to each disengagement theme.
5. Participants write down on yellow post-its possible reasons for staff engagement relative to each engagement theme.
6. Then, once finished, participants simply post their sticky notes on the walls of the seminar suite, clustering the groups' thoughts together.
7. Once everyone is finished, the participants then review the sticky notes and delete duplications and chunk the themes down into specific categories of drivers, e.g., leadership issues in relation to the greens or autonomous working in relation to the yellows.
8. The participants then transfer their findings onto a flip chart.
9. They then, in dialogue, allocate grading to each category in terms of their significance to create a hierarchy of categories.
10. Each group then presents to the wider group their findings, and the groups identify patterns and record these.

Closing frame

The closing frame is the stage in the day when the participants, with the aid of the facilitator, summarise their key learnings from the day. The facilitator then introduces the participants to an anonymous feedback app which acts as a back-channel that participants can use to anonymously comment, ask questions, or post their feedback about their learning from the dialogue seminar. The following day participants work in dialogue together to consider a model for moving forward to engage with key stakeholders in designing a change management intervention that helps address the weaknesses in staff engagement themes and builds upon associated strengths. The day ends with a final group dialogue to ascertain the group's commitment to investing their own and their teams' time into future, ongoing dialogue seminars to enable the change programme.

Conclusion

The aim of dialogue as we conceptualise it is to raise conscious awareness and to integrate perspectives to enrich leaders' understandings of organisational dynamics. The guiding principle comprises being open to examining assumptions, having one's thinking and beliefs challenged, and encouraging authentic self-expression of deep structure thinking. Through shared thinking, enabled by dialogue, participants enter the "I-Thou" relationship and break with the traditional "I-It" relationship synonymous with a transactional leadership culture based upon instrumental learning. This transition regarding the nature of self in relation to the other as a leader encourages the emergence of a conscious leadership culture and the enrichment of transactional leadership relationships. The aim is not to abolish instrumental learning; rather, the aim is to achieve a counterweight, that is, communicative learning. If an organisation can develop competencies that balance instrumental and communicative learning through a blended leadership model underpinned by a conscious leadership philosophy, then it can establish a source of competitive advantage. In the next chapter, we shall consider the role of coaching in facilitating such a change journey.

References

Argyris, C. (1971) Intervention Theory and Method: A Behavioural Science View. *Administrative Science Quarterly*, 16(4).

Argyris, C. & Schön, D.A. (1974) *Theory in Practice: Increasing Professional Effectiveness*. Jossey-Bass.

Dilts, R. (2003) *From Coach to Awakener*. Meta Publications.

Dixon, N.M. (1998) *Dialogue at Work*. Lemos & Crane.

11 CONSCIOUS LEADERSHIP COACHING

Introduction

This chapter considers the relationship between coaching and conscious leadership. To lead oneself and others with conscious awareness requires support to develop the skills required to achieve unconscious competence in this area of leadership practice. This support can be enabled by the learning and application of coaching capabilities both at the level of intrapersonal and interpersonal skills. For example, developing emotional management skills or improved decision-making skills are examples of intrapersonal coaching targets, whilst improving how one collaborates with followers would involve coaching, targeting interpersonal skills. The coaching process thus works with one's intra- and interpersonal skills. As successful conscious leadership is based upon effective management and mastery of our intra- and interpersonal skills, coaching is a highly relevant body of practice for the conscious leader to learn. This chapter considers the coaching approach inspired by the client-centred methods of Carl Rogers (1957) because of the emphasis on social relationships which underpin the quality of leadership membership exchange dynamics and outcomes.

Defining coaching

As with many social constructs, there is a wealth of diversity within the literature regarding how one can define coaching. The authors' definition of coaching is that: "Coaching involves a trained coach working with a client at the level of an individual, group or intergroup, to facilitate generative change at the level of values, beliefs, perceptions, behaviours and attitudes to enable the achievement of specific goals that are crafted as well-formed outcomes". It is important to note that the emphasis is placed upon the trained coach in this definition. Conscious leaders do benefit from formal training in coaching models and techniques. Coaching can be understood intellectually from books, although to "be a coach" requires the actual experience of practising coaching. The training room can provide a safe place for conscious leaders to learn coaching models, be introduced to coaching techniques and practice these with a training partner or with training groups. However, they will master such techniques through applied practice.

DOI: 10.4324/9781003272793-12

The inner coach

A core idea that our coaching philosophy orientates around is that whilst the conscious leader will benefit from the initial support of a qualified coach to train them regarding specific coaching models and skills; the main aim of this aspect of their personal development is to develop within the conscious leader their "inner coach". As previously mentioned, we all know that we have different identities or "identity parts" that we recognise in ourselves, such as the mother, the daughter, the son, the wife, the husband, the accountant, the colleague, the party animal, etc. These identity parts are our own and societies' cultural/social constructions. This means that as we go through our various life chapters, we accumulate additional identities; for example, the young man who self-identifies as a young man will one day, health allowing, recognise in himself the old man that he has become. In many ways, every culture in the world is based upon identity becoming, and many of these acquired identities can be understood as rites of passage, e.g., adolescent to adult. The conscious leader, therefore, must positively self-identify as a conscious leader and to do so, they need to act as a conscious leader; and, to do this, they need the skills and competencies of a conscious leader. They can facilitate this process by socially constructing a new part to their identity which we call their inner coach. The inner coach is the part of the conscious leader that acts as their "conscience", "teacher" and "awakener". The inner coach alerts the conscious leader as to when they need to access a high level of conscious awareness and the techniques they should employ at any given time to interact successfully as a conscious leader with their followers and with themselves.

The conscious leader can enjoy a reflective dialogue with their inner coach and re-run social experiences as if they were watching these on a movie screen, reflecting on these and, where required, reframing their initial interpretations and selecting alternative strategies for handling a similar situation when it occurs (Bandler and Grinder, 1982). For example, if the conscious leader has just delivered a presentation to their team and they felt, after the event, that they had not connected as positively with the team members as they would have liked, they could engage with their inner coach in a coaching dialogue and enact the following internal coaching session:

Self:	Well, that could have gone a lot better.
Inner coach:	What specifically could have gone a lot better?
Self:	The presentation . . . It was not what I wanted.
Inner coach:	What was it that specifically should have happened?
Self:	I wanted the team to be interested in what I had to say . . . to be motivated and energised.
Inner coach:	What does motivated and energised look or sound like or feel like to you?

Self:	People leaning in and listening, chatting enthusiastically, asking great questions, being positive.
Inner coach:	How were the people acting?
Self:	Quiet, a bit tense, they looked a bit unhappy, a bit remote from me as the leader.
Inner coach:	I can see how that would be very frustrating for you as I know how much you care about being a good and supportive leader to your team. What do you think would be generating those reactions in the group?
Self:	Umm . . . well . . . perhaps they were a bit taken aback, and maybe they just feel that with everything else going on, this was just another layer of hassle and stress.
Inner coach:	And how do you feel about your team feeling THAT way?
Self:	Well . . . I do not really blame them . . . I kind of understand . . . they have a lot going on now, and perhaps they are not as close to the situation as I am.
Inner coach:	It is good, is it not, that the team is understanding of the seriousness of the situation and the potential work involved?
Self:	Of course . . . absolutely
Inner coach:	So how will you build on that success as a leader and elicit feelings of confidence and optimism from your team going forward?
Self:	I think I will organise to meet with each of them individually to understand in more detail their perspective and look for opportunities for integrating our perspectives somehow and then meet again as a team to see how best we can all move forward.
Inner coach:	That's a really good strategy.

End of coaching session.

The above script had several coaching techniques imbedded in the narrative:

Framing: The inner coach initially helped the self to frame the social situation from their perspective. As we make sense of our experiences we have to organise, high volumes of empirical data. We socially construct selected sensory experiences into "interpretive frames of reference" enabled by our local culturally normative language. These "frames" can be considered as metaphors, i.e. as with a portrait in a frame. Our sense making interpretations are akin to paintings we frame and store in our memories. We assign meanings to these framed experiences, and these meanings influence our attitudes and, thus, our behaviours. This means that how we frame experience can be associated with the social results we generate through our interactions. It is important for conscious leadership that we are sensitive to the frames through which we make sense of and operate in the world around us, in particular for rapport purposes. If we can critically reflect on our framed experience and its content and functions, then we can intervene and socially reconstruct our frames of reference, change our attitudes and behavioural strategies and, thus, influence our social results.

Pacing Experience: This process involves respecting the way that others make sense of their experiences even when these differ from ones own. One does not have to agree with a persons perspective although it is important if one wishes to build rapport that you respect it. Dilts and DeLozier (2000, p. 910) define pacing as: "The process of using and feeding back key verbal and non-verbal cues from the other person in order to match his or her model of the world". You cannot "*lead*" another unless you are prepared to pace their experience. Pacing involves matching your experience of the world with that of the other.

Perceptual positioning: A technique that we can use as coaches to enable clients to work with reframing processes is that of perceptual positioning to build empathy (Dilts and DeLozier, 2000). At the heart of conscious leadership, one could suggest, lies the capacity for empathising and for critical reflexivity, which involves the ability to reflect upon one's own attitudes, decisions and behaviours in terms of how they impact our own lives, the lives of others and from the perspective of those we may hurt and those watching us in the moment and judging and, then, framing us. Perceptual positioning involves imprinting one's self into any one of three alternative perceptual positions.

First perceptual position

This state involves a person fully associating with their full sensory experience. It involves seeing, hearing and feeling from one's own perspective. This is the standard position we all adopt as we make sense of the world around us.

Second perceptual position

The second perceptual position involves the person "*stepping*" into the shoes of another person and fully associating with their emotional state, value and belief system, behavioural strategies and thinking strategies.

Third perceptual position

When we adopt the third perceptual position, we step into the shoes of an observer who can observe us interacting in the first perceptual position with another or with an event we must deal with. This enables us to gain insight from another perspective regarding how others see us.

In the sample of inner coaching provided above, the inner coach worked with both the first and second perceptual positions, which provide the self with multiple vantage points from which to perceive a phenomenon of interest and, thus, enrich their map of reality, thereby giving them greater sense-making resources. It also enables the development of empathy and greater rapport between potentially conflicting stakeholders.

Reframing: An important activity in which coaching practitioners engage in the practice of *"reframing"*, which we introduced in Chapter 2. Reframing can transform the experience of individuals and groups. The most effective way to explain reframing is by example. You can either change the content or the context of a framed situation, or you can change both. Detailed within the previous coaching transcript, the inner coach attended to shifting the nature of content framing from the self-viewing of the event as a leadership failure to an opportunity to build upon the leadership process. Further, the inner coach adopted the technique of "outcome reframing" when they invited the self to frame what a successful outcome would have been like.

Setting a well-formed goal: One of the desired outcomes of a coaching session is the establishment of a *"well-formed goal"*. A well-formed goal is a goal that has very clear criteria, e.g., the self-meeting with each member of their team to build upon the initial team meeting and establish an integrated perspective for moving forward. Coaching can also involve working externally from the self with individuals or groups.

Individual coaching compared with group coaching

Individual coaching involves a one-to-one coaching relationship whilst group coaching involves both coaching both individuals and groups. Individual coaching may involve facilitating substantial change for the client, whilst group coaching may also involve a deep change for group members. Group coaching sessions are generally longer than individual sessions mainly as a result of the number of individuals involved. Time allocations are also different as one on one coaching can last from 60 to 120 minutes whilst group coaching can last two to six hours and sometimes run over multiple days.

Similarities

Both one on one and group coaching situations will probably involve deep cultural changes in beliefs and values. In all cases the conscious leader as a coach is working to encourage an awakening process. (Dilts, 2003). A core coaching competence relative to both coaching situations is the practice of building empathy. A fundamental requirement of a coaching session is the willingness of participants to bring their COACH states and a genuine commitment towards personal and/or group change. Underpinning coaching as a key operating principle is the practice of self-directed learning. (Rogers, 1951). The coach does not advocate a solution to a client's problem, rather they facilitate reflective self-learning at the level of the individual, the group and the inter-group. Critical to all coaching approaches is the need for rapport to be established between the coach and their client, a coaching agreement agreed upon, clear goals established, action plans drafted, and performance indicators established and reviewed.

One can classify coaching in relation to 3 distinctive phases of development. Originally, we had the emergence of classic coaching which involved the coach prescribing the solution and the way forward for the client. This was followed by client centered coaching (Rogers, 1951) through which the coach acts as an awakener and a facilitator and so does not prescribe solutions. The client accesses their internal resources to establish the solution and the way. This is the main model that many coaching training programmes are based upon. Then a more contemporary model of coaching is generative coaching through which the coach and the client are in a shared dialogue and create a strong rapport based state relationship and from this dialogical relationship new integrated perspectives emerge that support the client. This stage can of course draw on the previous two stages in coaching development. The common principle to all coaching approaches is does it work and if it does then the coach can use any method that is ethically grounded in the service of their client. Flexibility of approach is required, and this involves constant study of the field of coaching and its developments to ensure one has a broad range of tools at ones disposal.

Explicit and implicit coaching

Explicit coaching can be understood as the operation of an actual formal coaching session with the clear purpose of enabling successful personal development. In an explicit coaching session, the time is pre-arranged, and a coaching agreement between the coach and client is prepared. The relationship between the coach and client is clearly defined. In contrast, an implicit coaching session can emerge in any leadership/followership dynamic and can be spontaneous and unplanned (Mayhead, 2020). In implicit coaching situations, the conscious leader uses coaching techniques to facilitate a successful outcome from a specific encounter with team members. For example, a team member may have concerns about managing a situation effectively, and the conscious leader informally coaches the team member through an introspective process to give them the confidence and internal resource they need. This may involve any one or more of the coaching techniques discussed in this chapter.

Theoretical grounding

The overarching theoretical approach that underpins conscious leadership coaching, as we understand it, is rooted in the theory of counselling known as "client-centred therapy", as developed by Carl Rogers (1957). Rogers' approach to counselling has subsequently been modelled throughout the global coaching community (Hutchinson, 2019). Rogers positions the concept of "self" or "self-concept" as central to the change process. Drawing on Rogers (1959), the self-concept is defined as: "The organized, consistent set of perceptions and beliefs about oneself". The self-concept has three key elements:

1. Self-worth, i.e., what we believe to be true about ourselves, which influences our self-esteem. Self-worth is influenced by our relationships with significant others and how they perceive us.
2. Self-image, i.e., how we see ourselves, the identities we assign to ourselves, and how we self-identify.
3. Ideal self, i.e., the person we aspire to be in life, which is closely connected to our goals and ambitions.

Often, there is tension between the three elements. Particularly, our ideal self and our sense of self-worth as informed by our interpretation of how significant others view us (Goffman, 1956). This state is known as incongruence and involves a mismatch between our ideal self and our experience with a lack of external identity validation on the part of significant others. In a typical coaching session, the aim may be to dissolve the state of incongruence and replace it with a more resourceful state of congruence, which involves strong feelings of self and external validation of the client's ideal self through positive reframing of elements of their social experiences (Haley and Arens, 1973).

The main emphasis and focus throughout a conscious leader coaching session are on the client's subjective maps of their world view in relation to their self-concept. The term "client" is a traditional appendage used in the coaching community to identify the recipient of a coaching service. An objective of coaching is to leverage the internal resources that the client has in order to establish more resourceful self-conceptions (Hutchinson, 2019). The role of the coach is to act as a guide and as an awakener (Dilts, 2003), to help the client generate new maps or new frames of reference regarding reflections on slices of social experience.

The client-centred approach puts emphasis on the client arriving at their own perceptual basis for personal change, which may involve a reframing of their worldview and their relationship to those in their social bubbles (Rogers, 1957). Essentially, the coaching approach adopts the principle that change comes from within the subjective world of the client; it is not imposed from outside by the coach. Rogers (1980, p. 115) states that: "Individuals have in themselves vast resources for self-understanding and for altering their self-concepts, basic attitudes, and self-directed behavior; these resources can be tapped if a definable climate of facilitative psychological attitudes can be provided". Therefore, the role of the conscious leadership coach is to enable personal change through a subjective reframing of beliefs that are limiting the self-actualisation potential of the client (Brause, 2004).

Carl Rogers was also a firm advocate for the self-actualisation of an individual's full potential (Maslow, 1954). Rogers fervently believed that individuals could grow, assuming they have the correct opportunities to do so, i.e., their environment provides acceptance of their potential and empathises with their desired need for personal growth and identity transformation. Rogers also insisted that, in order to self-actualise, people required clear goals aligned with the motivational desire to achieve these goals.

Identifying and reframing limiting beliefs

Beliefs drive our attitudes and behaviours and have a profound influence upon our framing of the self-concept and our social reality (Schein, 1985). Beliefs can be defined as: "Psychologically held understandings, premises, or propositions about the world that are felt to be true" (Richardson, 1996). A limiting belief is any belief that generates unproductive behaviours, emotions and attitudes that limit our ability to achieve desired social results. For example, a client may be holding on to limiting beliefs that need reframing. Reframing works with both content and context regarding the interpretive structure of the limiting belief. The coach applies creative questions to help the client identify any limiting beliefs and facilitate a reframing process to dissolve these and replace them with enabling beliefs.

Encouraging perceptual flexibility

Encouraging perceptual flexibility is a key coaching skill. Coaching can be understood as a form of dialogue between the coach and client. A kind of dialogue which aims to encourage the transition on the part of the client from a closed perspective to an open, then differentiated, and finally, an integrated perspective that dissolves limiting beliefs and encourages personal growth and development (Dixon, 1998). Also, the ability to develop a sense of how others view you is part of perceptual flexibility, and so the coach could encourage the client to adopt different stakeholder perceptual positions as part of the reframing process (Dilts, 2003).

Creative questioning

Creative questioning is the bedrock of a successful coaching session (Stoltz-fus, 2008). Hill (2004) claims that questioning, and the kind of questions presented, is central to supporting reflective learning on the part of the client in a coaching situation. The aim is to design questions that are ideally qualitative and open in nature and which generate introspective sense-making on the part of the client. Therefore, as an integral coaching method, the conscious leader as a coach designs several reflective questions which will enable the client to reflect deeply on the factors that are influencing their current framing of self and enable the reframing as required of the self-concept. Examples of such questions are presented in the inner coach sample provided previously.

Deep listening and backtracking

Deep listening and the related technique of backtracking are also key coaching skills, and the ability to listen authentically and demonstrate this via backtracking is a core coaching competence; it is also a skill. Backtracking involves: *"Reviewing or summarising, using another's key words and tonalities"* (O'Connor and Seymour, 2011, p. 229). Backtracking increases the confidence the client has in the coach, and it ensures that the coach is pacing the subjective world of the client effectively. Finally, honing our listening acuity and applying this capability actively in the coaching session will build trust with the client and impress upon them that they are being understood.

Designing well-formed goals

As discussed previously, developing a clear direction is a highly valuable outcome for a client undergoing the coaching process. Therefore, the coach would work with the client to design well-formed goals for the coaching session as well as post-coaching. The preferred definition of a well-formed goal is one which has been tested against a specific criterion. The criterion that tests the well-formed character of the coaching goals is the S.M.A.R.T. framework.

Conclusion

The aims of this chapter were to introduce the reader to the field of applied coaching and demonstrate the utility of coaching for successful conscious leadership. Team members will always have intra- and interpersonal issues, and the conscious leader as a coach can help them with these issues, which may involve a problem in respect to their personal identity, growth and development. The possession of coaching skills enhances the ability of the conscious leader to work with team members productively and encourages experiential and communicative learning. Coaching models and coaching philosophies also help the conscious leader work less from a functional ideology and more from a human-centric ideology. This chapter should be considered as a taster menu, a soft, albeit limited, introduction to the practice of coaching. However, the basic models and skills we have surveyed are excellent starting points for the conscious leader to develop, through practice and training, their conscious leadership coaching identity and capabilities. In the next chapter, we shall explore the principles of emotional intelligence and the development of the emotionally intelligent conscious leader.

References

Bandler, R. & Grinder, J. (1982) *Reframing*. Real People Press.

Brause, J. (2004) *How to Help Coaching Clients to Reframe Their Thinking, Effective Communication*. www.janbrause.co.uk/user/custom/downloads/HelpCoaching ClientsReframeTheirThinking.pdf.

Dixon, N.M. (1998) *Dialogue at Work*. Lemos & Crane.

Dilts, R. & Delozier, J. (2000) *Encyclopedia of Systematic Neuro-Linguistic Programming and NLP New Coding*. NLP University Press.

Dilts, R. (2003) *From Coach to Awakener*. Meta Publications.

Dilts, R. & Gilligan, S. (2021) *Generative Coaching Volume 1. The Journey of Creative and Sustainable Change*. I.A.G.C.

Goffman, E. (1956) *The Presentation of Self in Every Day Life*. Penguin Books.

Haley, J. & Arens, B. (1973) *Uncommon Therapy: The Psychiatric Techniques of Milton H. Erickson, M.D.* Echo Point Books.

Hill, P. (2004) *Concepts of Coaching: A Guide for Managers*. Institute of Leadership and Management.

Hutchinson, E. (2019) *Carl Rogers, Coaching & Mentoring*. www.eileenhutchinson.com/carl-rogers-coaching-mentoring/.

Maslow, H.A. (1954) *Motivation and Personality*, 3rd edn. Addison Wesley.

Mayhead, B. (2020) The Emergent Role of the Coaching Manager: An Experience of Working with IPA. *International Journal of Evidence Based Coaching and Mentoring. Series 14*, pp. 46–60.

O'Connor, J. & Seymour, J. (2011) *Introducing NLP: Psychological Skills for Understanding and Influencing People*. HarperCollins.

Richardson, V. (1996) The Role of Attitudes and Beliefs in Learning to Teach. In: J. Sikula (Ed.), *The Handbook of Research in Teacher Education*, 2nd edn. Macmillan, pp. 102–119.

Rogers, C.R. (1951) *Client-centred Therapy*, Kindle edn. Constable & Robinson.

Rogers, C.R. (1957) The Necessary and Sufficient Conditions of Therapeutic Personality Change. *Journal of Consulting Psychology*, 21(2), pp. 95–103.

Rogers, C.R. (1959) A Theory of Therapy, Personality, and Interpersonal Relationships: As Developed in the Client-Centered Framework. In: S. Koch (Ed.), *Psychology: A Study of a Science. Formulations of the Person and the Social Context*, vol. 3. McGraw Hill, pp. 184–256.

Rogers, C.R. (1980) *A Way of Being*. Houghton Mifflin.

Schein, H.E. (1985) *Organisational Culture and Leadership*. Jossey-Bass Publishers.

Stoltzfus, T. (2008) *Coaching Questions: A Coach's Guide to Powerful Asking Skills*. Coach 22.

12 THE EMOTIONALLY INTELLIGENT CONSCIOUS LEADER

Introduction

This chapter explores emotional intelligence as a key element of our conscious leadership model. Throughout this chapter, we define emotional intelligence (EI) with added emphasis upon defining emotional regulation (ER) and explain in detail its relationship with successful conscious leadership outcomes. We initially review some important research findings to establish a conceptual base for understanding EI. The principle that emotions are generated as a result of our reactions to others, i.e., "he made me angry", will be challenged; and we offer a counter-argument that advances the premise that we unconsciously choose our emotions, that they are social "strategies" we deliberately employ based upon cultural conventions. Finally, we conclude by establishing the case that emotions are internally generated states that drive our behaviour and interactions and, thus, have a significant emphasis upon our social results. We explore in detail the process of emotional regulation as a strategy that, if practised regularly, will help develop the quality and depth of our EI as conscious leaders.

What does the research tell us about EI?

We all know that, in general, those people who find themselves in executive leadership roles are bright. They have proved this by the fact that they have progressed in their careers and, most probably, passed exams to gain the required qualifications. However, we also know that leadership is not only a cognitive process; it is also a highly socially interactive and emotionally charged process. The leader needs to be able to work productively with other people and manage relationships in ways that build engagement and generate collaboration and trust. This requires an ability to develop not only one's intellectual IQ but also one's emotional EQ (Goleman, 1998).

Emotional intelligence implies an ability to meta reflect on our emotional states, meaning the ability to engage in a process of thinking, analysing, observing and reinterpreting the emotional states we generate in reaction to social events. The word "meta" is rooted in Greek and means "after" or "beyond".

DOI: 10.4324/9781003272793-13

Thus, EI involves a process of conscious awareness and intention to monitor our emotional states as they unfold and, when required, intervene and adjust these if they are impeding our ability to achieve our desired social results. The underlying theme of this definition is the premise that our emotions drive our behaviours, and so to change our behaviours, we must alter our emotions. In this sense, emotions can be considered as the batteries behind our social strategies, and, as such, they drive our behaviours and interactions and, thus, our social results.

Mayer et al. (2004, p. 197) define EI as: "The capacity to reason about emotions, and of emotions to enhance thinking. It includes the abilities to accurately perceive emotions, to access and generate emotions so as to assist thought, to understand emotions and emotional knowledge, and to reflectively regulate emotions so as to promote emotional and intellectual growth". Zeidner et al. (2009, p. 3) define EI as: "A generic competence in perceiving emotions (both in oneself and in others). This competence also helps us regulate emotions and cope effectively with emotive situations". Both definitions support and complement those previously discussed and indicate the idea that regulating emotional expression is a competency-based process. It is not an uncontrollable force that consumes us and one that we have no agency over; rather, emotional expressions are always our choice, whether they be conscious or unconscious expressions (Gross, 2001).

Emotions can also be understood as systems of communication (Russell and Barrett, 1999). Emotional intelligence, therefore, involves developing an increased sense of awareness regarding:

- One's own emotional states and what they mean to us.
- The way in which our emotional states are signalling meaning to others and affecting their emotions and behaviours.
- How our emotions are communicating with our body and generating our behaviours.
- How our emotions are communicating with our mind and generating our thoughts.

Goleman (1998) argues that EI can be developed, it can improve, and at an accelerated rate. However, for this improvement to happen, the conscious leader needs a framework to work with to guide such a deeply personal and introspective personal development journey, and this requires highly developed inter- and intrapersonal intelligence. Goleman (1998, p. 39) states that interpersonal intelligence includes: "The capacities to discern and respond appropriately to the moods, temperaments, motivations, and desires of other people". Intrapersonal intelligence he identifies as the key to self-knowledge, and he includes as a core intrapersonal competency: "Access to one's own feelings and the ability to discriminate among them and draw upon them to guide behaviour". Goleman has generated a useful framework for analysing the skills required to maintain and or develop one's EI capabilities which we describe below.

Self-awareness

This process involves paying attention to our feelings and our physical demeanour when involved in social interaction and treating these channels of expression as communication centres which can guide us more productively through our social interactions. External calibration involves taking a wider perspective, connecting through empathy with others to gain a closer evaluative experience of how they are feeling and acting in response to the signals we are giving off. These are critical conscious leadership capabilities.

Self-regulation

Self-regulation follows self-awareness and involves the monitoring and reframing of our sense-making interpretations and adjusting our emotional and physiological responses, as and when required, through a process of reappraisal; or, as this strategy is often referred to, reframing.

Motivating others

There is a close link implied by researchers such as Goleman (1998) and Gross (2001) between the emotive strategies we adopt and the ability to motivate and/or demotivate others and ourselves. If I, as a leader, bring elements of CRASH state into a social event with key stakeholders and they sense through my emotions and physiology that:

1. I am emotional tense or contracted;
2. I am perhaps physically or emotionally distant or separate from the group and its agenda;
3. I appear to be struggling to suppress how I am dealing with my emotions and holding on to my emotions from a positive place;

then, through the process of emotional contagions (Hatfield et al., 2014), they will likely intuitively model my state as the potential leader or, at the very least, the significant other in that moment for the group. When in CRASH state, we are not in a resourceful state. Thus, it is important that through self-awareness and subsequent emotional regulation through re-appraisal or reframing, we transition from a CRASH to COACH state before we enter the meeting and generate emotions associated with being connected with the group and the agenda; a sense of being open to the group's ideas and attentive to their needs whilst appearing centred and holding positive emotions, as this would be a far more motivating set of resources for the group.

Staying connected

The power of emotional contagions, which are based on the principle that people intuitively match the emotional states of significant others, can maintain powerful emotional connections within the group (Hatfield et al., 2014). Followers and leaders bond together through shared emotional states. Conscious leaders working through their emotional intelligence can calibrate (interpret) the emotional states of followers and match these and pace (not judge) these with a view to eliciting a required shift in emotional states on the part of followers, which is, itself, an act of leadership. This is the process of maintaining emotional rapport, and if the leader mismatches the emotional states of followers, they will break rapport and, subsequently, break the connection they have as leaders in relation to followers.

The ability model of EI

The ability to master one's intra- and interpersonal skills is largely dependent on one's ability to value and seek to develop one's emotional intelligence or EQ as well as one's IQ. Leaders need a balanced approach to developing IQ and EQ. Having one as a specific competency in the absence of the other will certainly weaken one's leadership potential. Emotions can be understood as systems of communication (Russell and Barrett, 1999).

Mayer et al. (2008) established their "Four Branch Model" of EI (see Figure 12.1), which incorporates four distinct branches of emotional expression that reflect many of the elements of the definitions previously reviewed.

To appreciate the logic behind this model we provide below a worked practical example of how it can be used as a system of emotional regulation.

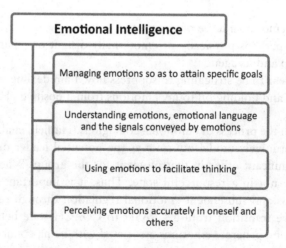

Figure 12.1 The Four Branch Model of Emotional Intelligence

Source: Mayer et al. (2008)

Managing emotions

A leader in an organisation is attending an operations meeting with a group of managers, some of whom are passionately against the leader's case for change. The leaders would, ideally, future pace the meeting, which involves imagining in advance how the social interactions would unfold. They would decide in advance what emotional state would best suit the social situation and anchor this state by associating it with a symbol that they associate with the emotional state. Then, when they enter into the actual meeting, they would connect with the anchor and elicit internally the emotional state they require, i.e., perhaps patience and understanding. This would constitute the first branch of the model.

Understanding emotions

When future pacing the event, the leader would empathise by taking the second perceptual position of audience members to understand their emotions and, importantly, the positive intentions that may be driving these emotions. They would look at the accessing cues such as body language, voice tone and facial expressions to gauge what the emotional states being demonstrated by their audience are signalling and how they are influencing individual and group behaviours. The leader would speculate as to the nature of the positive intention that these stakeholders may have that is supporting their emotional choices. This is the second branch of the model.

Using emotions strategically

As the leader interacts with their audience, they may start an internal dialogue with themselves and reflect on the emotional states they are generating and exhibiting and ask themselves some key reflective questions such as:

1. How am I feeling just now?
2. How do I feel about feeling this way?
3. Is this the most resourceful way for me to feel for myself and my audience?
4. How are my feelings of choice driving my behaviours?
5. Should I adopt a different emotional and behavioural state now?

This process of internal enquiry would constitute the third branch of the model.

Perceiving emotions

The fourth branch again emphasises self and social awareness and, importantly, sensory acuity, which refers to the leader's ability to use their senses to make accurate observations about themselves or other people. This process naturally involves the development of one's meta reflexivity (Alvesson et al., 2016).

The anthropological perspective

Within the discourse of anthropology, it is generally acknowledged that emotional expressions are, in fact, cultural expressions that are taught to cultural members through conscious and unconscious modelling of the significant others in society (Mesquita et al., 2016). Emotions, as we understand them from a social/cultural perspective, are actively constructed to meet the demands of the respective cultural environment. The contents and meanings of emotive expressions are shaped and influenced, often unconsciously, by the cultural expectations of our local culture. For example, different cultures will have different emotional strategies for responding to bereavement, celebrating, greeting, expressing unhappiness, or responding to an implied insult. The key lesson we take from these cultural facts is that our emotional responses are, in fact, social and, indeed, cultural constructions and are often hard-wired into our belief and value system; and, by being aware of the triggers and their meanings, we can consciously change our emotional responses by altering the meaning we attach to cultural triggers.

When making sense of our experience, we initially identify an attitude object (Maio et al., 2018) which is any perception of reality we construct in relation to a stimulus. For example, if a manager talks over a team member at a meeting with what the team member regards as a dismissive tone of voice, they would allocate a meaning against this attitude object, e.g., *"The manager does not respect me and has insulted me in front of my peers"*. This meaning construction subsequently becomes their frame of reference regarding the attitude object; it becomes their map of reality which the person embeds within their unconscious mind as a memory. The meaning they attribute towards the attitude object generates an emotional response which we can refer to as their "emotional state". The type of emotional response and its strength depends on the value the person places upon the attitude object and the meaning they attribute to it. The emotional state has a direct influence upon our behavioural state or behavioural strategy, and this impacts upon our social results. If we keep framing a social event the same way, the cycle of emotes, behaviour and social results derived from the process will become habitual. Our emotions do matter, and how we manage these as conscious leaders will have a significant influence on how successful we may be.

Different cultural groups at a national level will also have their own distinctive patterns of emotional responses. This principle equally applies to groups within organisations, especially to management teams. Mesquita et al. (2016, p. 4) claim that: *"Culturally normative emotions enable people to navigate the intricacies of their social environments in a coordinated fashion"*. Thus, we can assume that our emotions in use (our emotive strategies) are firmly connected to our values and beliefs regarding the extent we believe, culturally, that these emotions help to achieve the goals of the individuals, especially the group. A good example of this is the ritual of the Haka, through which New Zealand rugby players illicit a group emotional state combining courage, aggression and competitiveness to help the group win the game. The history of the haka pre-dates rugby and was traditionally the way a group of Maori warriors prepared for battle by eliciting a group emotionally shared state. Also, the haka can be used for peaceful reasons, e.g., to welcome guests and honour their presence and lived experiences; to elicit an intergroup shared emotional state of peace and harmony and inclusion.

Researchers have also confirmed that as people migrate across cultures, they also change, through time, their emotional strategies in use to match the new ethnic culture they are integrating into (Consedine et al., 2014), a process known as acculturation. In conclusion, from the cultural perspective, Mesquita et al. (2016, p. 10) assert that: Emotions are iterative and active constructions that help an individual achieve the central goals and tasks in a given (cultural) context. A key influencing skill, therefore, is mastering and matching the expression and appropriate selection of the emotional norms that cultural members of a group associate with effective group dynamics. However, this is not a straightforward affair as, often, our emotional repertoire is not only gifted to us by society, but is also unconsciously modelled from our parents. This means that we may, at times, react emotionally in ways that mismatch cultural convention in a corporate setting as we are intuitively selecting emotional strategies modelled from our parents as significant others (Blumer, 1969). Thus, EI involves meta-reflecting on the emotional habits we have adopted over time and consciously analysing these for their resourceful nature for both ourselves and for those we are interacting with and, when required, changing these. This process is known as emotional regulation.

Emotional regulation

Gross (2001, p. 215) frames the practices characteristic of EI as emotional regulation (ER), which he defines as: "Emotion regulation includes all of the conscious and non-conscious strategies we use to increase, to maintain or decrease one or more components of an emotional response. These components are the feelings, behaviours, and physiological responses that make up the emotion". Gross (2001) differentiates between emotional reappraisal and emotional suppression as two alternative emotional regulation methodologies. The former involves a series of tactics that we develop based on reflecting on a former experience and then employ before another similar social encounter takes place, and the latter is a series of tactics we activate in the emotional encounter. Both strategic approaches involve managing emotional content and behaviours with alert, conscious awareness.

Emotional regulation (ER) sits comfortably within our model of conscious leadership because, as regulatory strategies, they aim to review our emotional choices with conscious awareness and assess their utility as positive resources to enable the achievement of our social results. The aim of both ER and EI strategies as conscious leadership expressions is to ensure we do not emote and act out with conscious awareness. The question that Gross (2001) explores in his research is which group of strategies regarding ER are the most resourceful for the individual: emotional reappraisal or emotional suppression?

Reappraisal versus emotional suppression

For Gross (2001), emotional regulation through reappraisal is the most resourceful strategy for managing one's emotions with awareness. This is because, in contrast, and unlike reappraisal, emotional suppression absorbs energy; it takes considerable effort to try to suppress and even mask our emotional responses. For example, if a manager at a meeting thinks that a colleague or team member is deliberately resisting their influence, they may feel frustrated and perhaps even angry. If they choose to try to suppress these emotions, they will contract physically and may appear physically tense. The likelihood is that their inner emotional states will manifest through their tone of voice and their facial expressions, e.g., emotional leakage. They will most likely generate tense and frustrated energy, and there will be a lack of congruence between their masking and authentic inner states accessed through visual and auditory cues by their audience within the meeting room. Their blood pressure may rise and, overall, the quality of the social experience for all concerned will be poor.

Now, we all experience frustrated or even angry states. The principle of conscious leadership involves reflecting, post-event, on the resourceful nature of the suppression of emotional responses for both ourselves and for our team members, thereby identifying the triggers that elicited the internal emotional responses and establishing the meaning we have attributed to these triggers that generated the emotional responses. Subsequently, we can reappraise these meanings regarding what other, more resourceful meanings we could attribute to the triggers that would then elicit a more resourceful emotional response and associated body language, tonality, facial expression and energy.

Then, once we have reappraised or "reframed" the event and the key stimuli or triggers, we can imagine that we are back in that very social situation; yet, this time, we frame the triggers, or event, with the new reappraised meaning or reframe. We pay close attention to what we see, what we feel and what we hear. We elicit an emotional response congruent with the new frame of reference based on our reappraisal of the old frame. Then, we associate this emotional response and the frame of reference with a linguistic or physical symbol. For example, we may lightly touch our chest close to our heart as we experience positive emotions. This process we call anchoring (O'Connor and Seymour, 2011). We may practice this reframing and anchoring process several times. Then, when we next attend a management team meeting, we bring our new frame and anchor with us; and if and when the trigger reappears, we interpret it through the new frame of reference and "release" our anchor by touching our heart area on our chest and elicit the internally driven new emotional response.

By regulating the choice of emotional response with conscious awareness, conscious leaders maintain healthier rapport with followers and with peers. Importantly, we note that Person A could be adopting emotional suppression as their main emotional regulation strategy and, thus, weakening their rapport with potential followers and peers. They continue to do this outwith conscious awareness. If exposed to experiential-led training regarding the conscious leadership model outlined throughout this book, they can learn to differentiate between leading consciously and trying to lead without conscious awareness. They can learn to differentiate between habitually adopting reappraisal or suppression-driven emotional regulation strategies in order to make an informed choice. If person A then switches from relying upon emotional suppression as an emotional regulation strategy to reappraisal as their habitual choice, then the rapport levels with their potential followers and peers should start to improve; rapport is a critical element in effective leadership outcomes.

Closing exercise

Identify a time when you were to chair a meeting or deliver a presentation, or even attend an interview when you were not, on reflection, in a resourceful state. You may have felt that you were a bit stressed or anxious or some other kind of emotional state that got in the way of you being at the very best of your potential for the event. Using the technique of reappraisal, meta reflect on the event of your choice and reframe aspects of the content that may be stimulating negative thoughts and energy. Then, reflect on how this method of reflection may help you in your career. Use the following method to guide your reframing process:

1. What was the nature of the activating event that triggered your emotional response, and how would you describe your feelings?
2. What were the core beliefs you associated with the activating event that triggered your emotional responses?
3. What were the consequences for you adopting the emotional response you chose?
4. If you were to reframe the beliefs you associated with the activating event, i.e., dispute these, how could you reframe these?
5. How does this reframing of the original beliefs influence or change the energy you feel emotionally towards the activating event?

Conclusion

The aims of this chapter were to introduce the reader to the concept of emotional intelligence and its utility for developing our conscious leadership skills. Emotional intelligence is simply a competency-based construct. It is a human characteristic that can be developed; it is not something that we are born with as a fixed amount, with some people having more EI than others.

With practice, mediated by some simple techniques, we can all develop the standard and effectiveness of our emotional intelligence. When we combine emotional intelligence with cognitive and social intelligence, we become far more rounded as human beings, especially as leaders. It is difficult to conceive of effective leadership if the potential leader lacks a resourceful depth of emotional intelligence. This is because emotional intelligence is closely linked to building rapport through matching and pacing the experience of followers. It is a critical mediator of effective and enriching leadership/membership exchanges both at the level of the dyad and of the group. Emotional intelligence is a primer for developing psychological safety in teams as an act of conscious leadership which shall be the topic of the next chapter, e.g., psychological safety and conscious leadership.

References

Alvesson, M. & Spicer, A. (2016) *The Stupidity Paradox: The Power and Pitfalls of Functional Stupidity at Work*. Profile Books.

Blumer, H. (1969) *Symbolic Interactionism*. University of California Press.

Consedine, S.N., Magai, C. & Bonanno, A.G. (2014) Moderators of the Emotion Inhibition-Health Relationship: A Review and Research Agenda. *Review of General Psychology*, 6(2), pp. 204–228.

Goleman, D. (1998) *Working with Emotional Intelligence*. Bantam Books.

Gross, J.J. (2001) Emotion Regulation in Adulthood: Timing Is Everything. *Current Directions in Psychological Science*, 10, pp. 214–219.

Hatfield, E., Bensman, L., Thornton, D.P. & Rapson, L.R. (2014) New Perspectives on Emotional Contagion: A Review of Classic and Recent Research on Facial Mimicry and Contagion. *Interpersona*, 8.

Maio, R.G., Haddock, G. & Verplanken, B. (2018) *The Psychology of Attitudes and Attitude Change*. Sage.

Mayer, J.D., Salovey, P. & Caruso, D.R. (2004) Emotional Intelligence: Theory, Findings, and Implications. *Psychological Inquiry*, 15, pp. 197–215.

Mayer, J.D., Salovey, P. & Caruso, D.R. (2008) Emotional Intelligence: New Ability or Eclectic Traits? *American Psychologist*, 63(6), pp. 503–517.

Mesquita, B., Boiger, M. & De Leersnyder, J. (2016) The Cultural Construction of Emotions. *Current Opinion in Psychology*, 8, pp. 31–36.

O'Connor, J. & Seymour, J. (2011) *Introducing NLP: Psychological Skills for Understanding and Influencing People*. HarperCollins.

Russell, J. & Barrett, L. (1999) Core Affect, Prototypical Emotional Episodes, and Other Things Called Emotion: Dissecting the Elephant. *Journal of Personality and Social Psychology*, 76, pp. 805–819.

Zeidner, M., Matthews, G. & Roberts, R.D. (2009) *What We Know About Emotional Intelligence: How It Affects Learning, Work, Relationships, and Our Mental Health*. MIT Press.

13 CONSCIOUS LEADERSHIP AND PSYCHOLOGICAL SAFETY

Introduction

In this chapter, we review the concept of psychological safety, drawing inspiration from important research papers. We start with a review of definitions of psychological safety from the perspective of relevant scholars, and we identify the main blockers of psychological safety. The clear connection between the emergence of psychological safety with conscious leadership practices is discussed. Responding to key research findings and contributions from scholars, we describe characteristics of practice that conscious leaders may adopt to facilitate with conscious awareness the creation of a culture that supports the manifestation of psychological safety in both individuals and groups. Drawing inspiration from the ideas of Rosabeth Kanter (2013), specifically her Six Keys to Leading Positive Change, we illuminate key characteristics of behaviours that support the emergence of a psychologically safe workplace. Building on the Six Keys to Leading Positive Change framework, we then discuss the utility of coaching methods and ideas, inclusive of state management, to enable psychological safety in groups. The sensitive function of providing feedback and how this influences the emergence of psychological safety is then reviewed.

Defining psychological safety

The concept of psychological safety was brought to current prominence by Edmondson (1999) when she published her findings and ideas in an article called "Psychological Safety and Learning Behaviour in Work Teams", published in *Administrative Science Quarterly*. In this research paper, Edmondson studies the connection between psychological safety and the emergence of successful team learning and establishes a highly influential relationship between the two outcomes. Essentially, Edmondson was interested in understanding: "The factors that influence learning behaviour in ongoing teams in real organizations" (1999, p. 350). Central to her studies were cognitive and interpersonal factors, especially the tacit beliefs about risk taking in interpersonal interactions. Edmondson (1999, p. 353) was especially interested in contributing towards our knowledge of the: "Role of beliefs about the interpersonal

DOI: 10.4324/9781003272793-14

context in individuals' willingness to engage in otherwise-threatening learning behaviour". Edmondson identifies the importance of factors such as cultural context, leadership coaching and the generation of positive shared meaning systems as being supportive of building a climate of interpersonal trust and risk taking and, therefore, key drivers of psychological safety.

A main blocker of the emergence of psychological safety identified by Edmondson was the protection of "face", i.e., losing credibility in front of one's peers by admitting a mistake, asking a question that may reveal one's ignorance, or simply asking a colleague's opinion about a problem in one's area of responsibility. These blockers of self and group learning clearly impair the capacity for leveraging collective intelligence through collaborative problem solving and insulate powerful silos throughout the organisation. Therefore, even though such defensive behaviours may seem highly counterintuitive as they restrict the growth of the individual, the group and the organisation, they also generate powerful secondary gains; they protect the individual from the threat of embarrassment.

Prior to Edmondson's research into psychological safety, the scholar Kahn (1990, p. 708) defined psychological safety as a state of: "Being able to show and employ one's self without fear of negative consequences of self-image, status or career". It is understood that when leaders create a field of psychological safety, staff engagement increases significantly. Edmondson (1999, p. 6) defines psychological safety within a group setting as: "a shared belief that the team is safe for interpersonal risk taking".

Edmondson highlights several examples (see Table 13.1) in different organisations of how mistakes were made and not acknowledged or confronted. The driving force behind this cultural norm of resisting the acknowledgement of mistakes is a fear of looking incompetent. Edmondson arrived at the following psychological drivers that maintained individual and group insecurity and anxiety regarding open dialogue:

Table 13.1 Drivers that weaken dialogue

No One Wants To Look:	It's Easy to Manage if We:
Ignorant	Don't ask questions
Incompetent	Don't admit weaknesses or mistakes
Intrusive	Don't offer ideas
Negative	Don't critique the status quo

The above translates into an impression management strategy which is highly effective at protecting one's self-image and at diluting the potential for personal and group development and organisational innovation through appreciative enquiry and team learning. However, Edmondson is optimistic and claims that there are examples of organisations which create a culture of psychological safety to encourage team members to speak up and express themselves, to ask questions without fear of penalty, challenge cultural norms and not always simply go with the flow; they encourage individual and team reflexivity. These organisations are encouraging the emergence of the learning organisation enabled through the establishment of a generative field of psychological safety in groups as the difference that made the difference in producing high-performance teams.

Connecting conscious leadership with psychological safety

To lead with conscious awareness and encourage others to model your conscious leadership traits requires the support of a psychologically safe work climate, i.e., a culture of psychological safety. Reflexivity at the level of both the individual and the group encourages the manifestation of psychological safety and the manifestation of reflexive practices as a means of learning. A culture of leadership that is genuinely distributed throughout the group should be based upon the archetypical conscious leadership model expressed by the team leader. The conscious leadership culture should be characterised by psychological safety, strong group resilience, high levels of rapport and, the glue that holds this model together, highly developed emotional intelligence as a fundamental leadership competence. Individual and team learning are based on critical reflexivity. This process naturally involves transitioning from a closed to open perspective to consider alternative views, and this enables the adoption of a differentiated and, finally, an integrated perspective: the final product of learning. The philosopher John Dewey (1922) described learning as a frequently evoked process of reflecting upon and, when required, modifying actions. The process of transitioning from a culture of impoverished transactional leadership to one that is enriching with transformational motivational resources embedded in the leadership culture, clearly, is a highly reflective personal and group learning process.

Conscious leadership practices are, by their very nature, highly revealing in terms of our areas of personal development and growth that are always experiencing transition. Conscious leadership development depends on a willingness to take intra- and interpersonal risks, which can threaten one's ideal self-conception. It is quite challenging to imagine a culture of conscious leadership emerging against an organisational backdrop characterised by low levels of psychological safety. Therefore, the role of the executive team, if they are committed to building a culture of conscious leadership, is to commit to also building a supporting generative field of psychological safety. The next section provides a framework through which psychological safety may be built through conscious leadership collaboration within a leadership team using a group coach.

How to build psychological safety with conscious awareness

A useful model Rosabeth Moss Kanter (2013) has developed that could frame an intervention into the dynamics of the team with the aim of establishing a higher quality of psychological safety, is what she refers to as the Six Keys to Leading Positive Change. Each key is, basically, a principle that a management team should base its leadership culture upon. For example:

1. **Show up:** When you attend a meeting with the team, be truly present intellectually, emotionally and attentively.
2. **Speak up:** Be vocal and use your voice to generate new perspectives and encourage the building of dialogue.
3. **Look up:** Encourage the dreamer as well as the realist in the team. Give a voice to your vision and demonstrate your ability to chunk down into the detail and chunk up into the future.
4. **Team up:** Build solid collaborative connections with your colleagues; be open to their feedback and welcome this as a positive resource.
5. **Never give up:** Be highly flexible; perceive setbacks as feedback loops and learning opportunities to keep progressing.
6. **Lift others up:** Role model the above qualities; coach and inspire team members to higher levels of psychological safety and performance.

Psychological safety enabled through coaching

Professor Kanter's insightful model of the Six Keys to Leading Positive Change can be used to frame a conscious leadership intervention which aims to develop psychological safety in a team. The intervention could be facilitated with dialogue seminars to explore and discuss what each change key means to each person. In Chapter 11, we discussed the principles of building coaching competencies within a leadership team so that, ultimately, conscious leaders may function as self-coaches. Initially, the conscious leader functioning as the team coach could meet with each team member to explore what each change key means to them and what they think enables or hinders them from actively modelling each of the six change keys as leaders. The coach would classify the themes identified by the participant as either "blockers" or "enablers" of psychological safety relative to each change key. For example, regarding "speaking up", an enabler might be: "Speaking about a subject that is in my area of responsibility", and a blocker might be: "I don't want to step on anyone's toes". The coach would then analyse the responses from all team members and look for patterns and remove duplications to create distinctive categories of blockers and enablers of psychological safety that the team members recognised in the coaching sessions.

COACH state

As part of the coaching sessions, the coach could discuss with each team member the principles of COACH state (see Chapter 1) and explain how accessing COACH state at an individual and group level increases feelings of psychological safety in a group. As stated in Chapter 1, the COACH state model of coaching was developed by Robert Dilts and his colleague Stephen Gilligan, two California-based behavioural change experts, to help their clients recognise un-resourceful states and elicit internally generated resourceful states to enhance their social performance. Eliciting an individual and group COACH state as a primer before the dialogue seminar starts is one very productive and relatively straightforward body of applied practice that encourages dialogue.

Coaching container

As part of the coaching session, the coach could introduce the idea of reframing the meeting space as a "coaching container" (Dilts, 2003). This new frame involves perceiving the dialogue seminar as an experimental space: a space of creativity, learning, reflection and self and group development. In this space, each team member is responsible for modelling the six change keys as specific behaviours and attitudes and for mutual coaching. This is a coaching container where new behaviours are developed and internalised and where participants can open up and share their thoughts and concerns free from fear of ridicule or chastisement, the essence of psychological safety.

Recognising CRASH state

Another key element of the coaching session is to raise the conscious awareness of the participants of CRASH state and to help them recognise its manifestation in themselves and in colleagues. The aim of this coaching moment is to improve upon the participants' ability to adopt mindfulness in relation to their inner states at any moment. For example, if I tune into my capability for self-awareness or mindfulness regarding my internal states, I can "notice" when I am entering or have entered CRASH state and am perhaps struggling to hold challenging feelings resourcefully. For example, the emotional state of anxiety that is flooding through me for whatever reason. I can also feel my body's physical reaction as I tense up and contract. There is a simple exercise inspired by the work of Robert Dilts that we can use as conscious leaders to identify if we are in CRASH state or COACH state, and the following is a transcript from a self-coaching exercise conducted by one of the authors as an example prior to joining an important meeting:

> "How am I feeling just now?"
> "Uptight and anxious".
> "How is my body responding to these emotions?"
> "I am contracting and tensing, moving towards defensive body language".
> "How do I feel about feeling that way?"
> "Not very happy".

"What is it about the meeting that I am focusing in upon that is making me unhappy?"

"I am concerned some of the participants will mock me if I open up and share my feelings".

"What else could I focus upon going into this meeting that would be more resourceful for me and for everyone else?"

"I could focus in on the opportunity to engage with everyone, to share my enthusiasm and optimism".

"So that is what I am going to do . . . excellent . . . how does the idea of applying that strategy make me feel now?"

"Calmer, more certain and confident . . . quite relaxed".

The above technique is a self-coaching method that can be used to practice self-reflection and, thus, improve upon one's emotional intelligence competencies and elicit a transition from CRASH to COACH states or to strengthen COACH state. It is a reframing method rooted in mindfulness, which will break the pattern of experiencing repetitive behaviours and emotions that are not proving resourceful for you or for strengthening those which are.

Feedback and psychological safety

The literature on Leadership Membership Exchange (LMX) dynamics clearly points towards the importance of team member feedback and the emergence of psychological safety (Van den Berg, 2010). Rather than provide feedback unreflectively redundant of any sense of conscious awareness, organisations need to learn how to manage the process of providing feedback so as not to dilute the quality of psychological safety but encourage individual and group learning. An interesting idea, borrowed from the personal development movement and the coaching movement (Dilts and Delozier, 2000), is reframing failure as feedback with the belief that there is no failure, only feedback. This reframe ensures that the learning loop is kept open and is not closed prematurely. It also encourages the growth of psychological safety in individuals, dyads, groups and inter-groups and, thus, enables rapport and learning. However, researchers such as Cannon and Edmondson (2005) claim that such a practice, being open to treating failures as opportunities for learning in organisations, is, in fact, rare.

Edmondson (1999, p. 8) claims that: "If the leader is supportive, coaching-oriented, and has non-defensive responses to questions and challenges, members are likely to conclude that the team constitutes a safe environment". The traits Edmondson is citing here are clearly social skills or soft skills that can be learned and developed with conscious awareness. In contrast to the coaching style Edmondson also claims that: "In contrast, if team leaders act in authoritarian or punitive ways, team members may be reluctant to engage in the interpersonal risk involved in learning behaviors such as discussing errors". The traits she indicates here also are clearly ones that can be associated with our model of anti-conscious leadership based upon the impoverished transactional style of LMX dynamics introduced in Chapter 7.

A significant element of learning and LMX dynamics is the way in which feedback is provided. If one were to adopt the reframe that there is no failure, only feedback, then how would a leader provide feedback to a team member? The first thing is for the leader to adopt intentional language choices when providing feedback (Omilion-Hodges and Ptacek, 2021) which involves the careful framing of the structure of the feedback linguistically and also paying attention to the tonality used and the style of body language exhibited during the LMX feedback moment. We know from the seminal research of Albert Mehrabian (1971) that when involved in a discussion regarding a subject which has high emotional valence, the receiver of the intended message will make sense of it based on 7% attention to the actual words used, 38% to tonality and 55% to facial expressions and body language. Thus, tonality and body language are far greater signifiers of meaning than the actual words employed. The tone of voice we use and how we express ourselves physically when delivering sensitive messages really does matter. It is often the case that highly influential people such as managers or leaders may deliver feedback that involves constructive criticism without any conscious awareness, thereby resulting in counterproductive outcomes.

Giving fish and stretch

Drawing once more from the personal development movement, we can illustrate a very productive way to provide feedback which has the potential to enhance psychological safety in dyads, groups and inter-groups and reduce the risk of counterproductive outcomes such as even weaker rapport, lack of trust and the harbouring of grievances between leaders and their team members. The feedback model is known as "providing Fish and Stretch" (Dilts, 2003). The idea of giving fish provides us with a way to reframe feedback moments. By focusing on the strengths in someone's work or behaviours and acknowledging these, we can preserve the status of psychological safety and perhaps even strengthen it between the leader and the team member. For example, if a team member delivers a presentation and their leader only points out opportunities to improve upon the presentation and the delivery style, this is an example of someone embedded in a narrow judgemental perspective based on their maps of best practice. This approach reduces psychological safety and rapport between the leader and their team member.

This is not to say that errors should be ignored; rather, if this is the only feedback offered, it will not encourage rapport-building and the emergence of psychological safety in LMX relationships. Thus, it is good practice to learn how to empathise the strengths in the presentation and its delivery, which we refer to as providing fish, and then, once rapport is established, the leader can provide "stretch", which is an opportunity for the learner (the team member) to reflect and to develop.

Intentional language style; giving fish and stretch

The careful framing of feedback statements should be practised by the leader providing any feedback to team members using an intentional language style such as:

> "What I observed in your performance was . . ."
> "What I really liked about it was . . ."
> "What you did that I really appreciated was . . ."
> "The reason that I really appreciated it was because . . ."
> "For me, what was particularly impressive about your performance was . . ."
> "The reason for this was . . ."

The above statements are examples of fish.

These language patterns help to demonstrate the value the leader places on a team members strengths. Leaders sometimes must "stretch" the competencies of members of their team, and they can do so using the following linguistic patterns:

> "What I observed that could be further developed was . . ."
> "The reason for this is . . ."
> "I really liked when you . . . and if you were to . . . I think it could be even more effective".
> "The reason for this is . . ."
> "When you . . . what I noticed was . . . and if you . . . I think you would . . ."
> "The reason for this is . . ."

These intentional language strategies should always be expressed authentically, and when done this way, they can function as highly dynamic engagement catalysts stimulating rapport with both leaders and their team members and encouraging psychological safety.

Conclusion

Psychological safety has been long recognised as a significant enabler of organisational development and learning at the level of the individual, group and inter-group (Schein and Bennis, 1965). If a leadership culture is based upon an impoverished transactional model, then it is safe to assume that rapport between leaders and followers will be weak or non-existent. This lack of rapport may also signify a lack of reflexivity on the part of team leaders regarding their contribution to the lack of rapport. This lack of reflexivity reduces the opportunity for personal development and learning. Learning operates at several levels, e.g., cognitive, emotional and behavioural. If there is a lack of personal reflexivity and line management/staff relations are based on weak rapport and possibly management by exemption, active or passive,

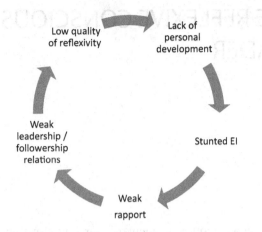

Figure 13.1 Cycle of Failure to Establish Psychological Safety in Groups

then opportunities to develop one's emotional intelligence as a leader are also stunted. This creates a vicious cycle leading to the blocking of the emergence of psychological safety, as illustrated in Figure 13.1.

The role of a conscious leader is to break this vicious cycle and create an alternative which generates a healthy and vibrant climate of psychological safety within a team. This process involves, in no small measure, reflexivity, which is the subject of the next chapter.

References

Cannon, M. & Edmondson, A. (2005) *Failing to Learn and Learning to Fail (Intelligently): How Great Organizations Put Failure to Work to Innovate and Improve.* Long Range Planning.

Dewey, J. (1922) *Human Nature and Conduct: An Introduction to Social Psychology.* Henry Holt and Company.

Dilts, R. (2003) *From Coach to Awakener.* Meta Publications.

Dilts, R. & Delozier, J. (2000) *Encyclopedia of Systematic Neuro-Linguistic Programming and NLP New Coding.* NLP University Press.

Edmondson, A. (1999) Psychological Safety and Learning Behavior in Work Teams. *Administrative Science Quarterly*, 44(2), pp. 350–383.

Kahn, W.A. (1990) Psychological Conditions of Personal Engagement and Disengagement at Work. *Academy of Management Journal*, 33, pp. 692–724.

Kanter, R.M. (2013) *Six Keys to Positive Change.* TED Talk. https://conorneill.com/2016/07/06/6-keys-to-leading-positive-change-rosabeth-moss-kanter/.

Mehrabian, A. (1971) *Silent Messages*, 1st edn. Wadsworth. ISBN 0-534-00910-7.

Omilion-Hodges, L. & Ptacek, J. (2021) *What Is the Leader – Member Exchange (LMX) Theory?* Palgrave Macmillan.

Schein, E.H. & Bennis, W.G. (1965) *Personal and Organizational Change Through Group Methods: The Laboratory Approach.* Wiley.

Van den Berg, P. (2010) Stimulating Knowledge Sharing by Error Management and Leader-Member Exchange. *Journal of Intellectual Disability Research*, 8(2).

14 THE REFLEXIVE CONSCIOUS LEADER

Introduction

This chapter reviews another element of our conscious leadership model, which is reflexivity. Reflexivity involves more than reflecting upon a prior experience; it involves analysing and interpreting with acute focus our experience of past events and the role that our beliefs, values, ideas, vocabulary, emotions and behaviours play in generating our social results. Reflexivity, as we understand it and employ it within our model of conscious leadership, is a fundamental self-development technique. We compare reflective practices with reflexive practice and demonstrate how both intervention methods can be used to raise our conscious awareness as leaders of the incongruence between our theories of action and our theories in action. We introduce some exercises that can enable reflexivity.

Defining reflexivity

Reflexivity is a very specific form of reflection with a unique function that separates it from other modes of reflective practice. By reflexivity, we relate to the definition provided by Alvesson et al. (2017, p. 14) as: "The ambition to carefully and systematically take a critical view of one's own assumptions, ideas, and favoured vocabulary and to consider if alternative ones make sense". We can best explain the characteristics of reflexivity by comparing the practice against other modes of reflective practice that are not specifically reflexive in nature in relation to the previous definition.

Reflexivity is closely related to "reflection", which Alvesson et al. (2017, p. 13) define as: "An important human activity in which people recapture their experience, think about it, mull it over and evaluate it". Reflection as a subset of reflexivity is therefore considered to be a critical leadership skill and one that can be improved upon by daily practice. Schön (1983) points us towards reflection "on action" and reflection "in action"; the former is reflecting after we act, and the latter is reflecting as we act. Self-reflection, whether "on" or "after", is an important means for personal development and learning on the part of the leader; however, it does need the additional discipline of enhanced self-awareness and making reflective practice a habit. Reflexivity

DOI: 10.4324/9781003272793-15

differs from reflection as it involves deeper introspective enquiry on the part of the reflexive leader. Greenwood (1998, p. 1049) also identifies "reflection before action", which: "Involves thinking through what one wants to do and how one intends to do it before one actually does it". Thus, reflection can be understood as consisting of three dimensions (see Figure 14.1):

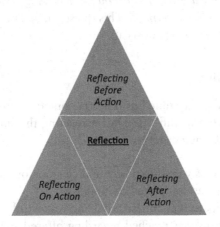

Figure 14.1 Three Dimensions of Reflecting

We leave the final definition of reflexivity to Alvesson et al. (2017, p. 14), who state that: "Reflexivity means a willingness to scrutinise and challenge one's position-image-, sense-making and vocabulary on a subject matter (such as one's work and one's self) and consider alternative position".

Surface structure reflection

Surface-level reflection is a branch of reflective practice which focuses on basic recall of an event based upon our initial interpretation. This is basic memory recall. Alvesson et al. (2017) regard this kind of reflective practice as a standard reflex. For example, I may attend a meeting and I am asked: "*How did the meeting go?*" I pause as the question triggers surface-level reflection and I describe the main features that come to mind, for example: "*Yes, it went fine . . . people looked engaged and we made good progress*". This level of reflection is shorthand for describing an experience at a thin level of detail, and it is an essential communicative tool that makes the machinery of social interaction practically efficient.

Mid-level structure reflection

Mid-level structure reflection is a branch of reflective practice that involves chunking down to explore more details that underpin the surface level reflections. For example, in our imaginary conversation, my conversational partner was a business researcher studying team dynamics in management meetings, and they asked, "*What aspects of the meeting went particularly well for you, and, I am curious, what does engaged mean to you personally?*" This question invites, by necessity, mid-level reflective practice. I need to focus with greater depth on the experiences that I had and the interpretations of these experiences that generated the surface-level reflective description. And if, after I had replied, the researcher was to ask, "*You said 'we made good progress' . . . can I ask you what specifically is your criteria for achieving good progress and how did this manifest in your meeting?*" This question, again, keeps my reflective focus at a mid-level of analytical recall.

Deep level reflexivity

Deep level reflexivity is a branch of reflective practice. For example, let's say one's criteria for what qualifies as a team meeting that made good progress consisted of the following criteria:

- All agenda items were discussed, and clear actions agreed upon.
- The meeting was completed on time.
- Every participant was cordial, civil and respectful.
- Team consensus was reached regarding offered solutions to problems raised.
- Everyone was engaged and contributed to the meeting.

Reflexive practice would invite the following questions in relation to one's criteria:

- Is there any other criterion I could refer to that I don't when evaluating the progress of my meetings?
- Why do I value each criterion I have identified above?
- What are the core beliefs that I hold that produce my motivation to value these criteria?
- How would I feel if one or more of these criteria were not met?
- Do I understand what criterion my colleagues would have that represents a progressive meeting from their perspectives?
- If I think I do understand their criterion, how do I know that I know this?
- What do I do in terms of behaviour to manage the outcomes within the meeting to meet my criteria?
- What kind of reflective practice do I encourage in the meeting?
- Am I encouraging thinking in the moment, in the past, in the future or elements of all three thinking strategies?
- If I encourage one thinking style over others, why do I do this, and what is the opportunity cost of doing this?
- How do I react to participants asking challenging questions?
- Why do I react that way?
- How else could I facilitate the team meeting?

- Are we assuming that our way is the right way, the only way to manage team meetings?

The above questions invite deep structure critical reflection regarding the beliefs, values, vocabulary, thinking styles, perceptual positions, behavioural and emotive and identity constructs that the reflexive leader draws upon to manage a progressive team meeting from their perspective.

Reflexivity, as we understand it and employ it within our model of conscious leadership, is a fundamental self-development technique. Reflexive practice can enable conscious leaders to learn from personal experience. Therefore, we are, when engaging in reflexive practice, deliberately placing our belief systems into a temporary state of insecurity and doubt, and the aim is to explore if alternative options make sense. As Alvesson et al. (2017) state, reflexivity involves: "Interpretations of our interpretations", e.g., deep structure thinking and, specifically, as the questions above indicate, interpretations of the values and beliefs that influenced our original reflective frames of reference at both surface and mid-level reflection and the behaviours and emotions we generated as a result of these initial interpretations. Alvesson et al. (2017) also call this process *"meta reflection"*, i.e., thinking about thinking, especially how we are thinking, and the beliefs and values that drive a particular thinking strategy.

Reflexivity is a critical practice during periods of cultural change in an organisation when cultural orthodoxy maintained through a rigid system of beliefs, values and cultural norms of behaving, thinking and emoting are being scrutinised and challenged. This is the focus of conscious leadership, and it is this focus and commitment to reflexive practice that, at its core, defines conscious leadership as a distinctive branch of leadership in general.

A significant aspect of reflexive practice, as a conscious leader, involves perceptual flexibility: a willingness to adopt perspectives other than our own. For example, stepping into the shoes of other team participants and making sense of the meeting in terms of their criteria, which we call taking the second perceptual position. We may also adopt the third perceptual position, which involves assuming the role of an objective outsider who is watching us manage the team meeting. Thus, a significant reflexive capability is perceptual agility and the ability to hold all three perspectives from a resourceful intellectual and emotional space as part of the reflexive process.

Reflexive practice facilitates a process of awakening the gaps in our knowledge regarding how our own thinking styles, emotions and behaviours influence the production and maintenance of organisational practices and why such practices might generate stakeholder disengagement.

Tools for facilitating reflexivity in conscious leaders

An effective tool for encouraging reflexivity in a leadership team is to invite participants to be reflexive regarding their operating philosophy as leaders. All leaders will hold, often at an unconscious level, an operating philosophy regarding the nature of leadership and, indeed, management. This idea is well documented and has been researched substantially. For example, Douglas McGregor (1960) wrote his ground-breaking book The Human Side of Enterprise, which essentially compared two opposite leadership/management philosophies: Theory X and Theory Y.

When a leader is presented with an articulation of a leadership philosophy that is a mismatch with their own, this mismatch triggers a process of reflection which can lead to reflexivity by reviewing, critically, the philosophy and related practice of conscious leadership that we relate to. A philosophical framework that can be employed to facilitate such a reflexive process is drawn from the field of personal improvement (Tosey and Mathison, 2009) and is based upon the following core beliefs:

1. *The map is not the territory* (How we perceive a situation does not reflect the concrete truth; it is only our map, and other maps will be different).
2. *Take responsibility for your social results* (it is my behaviour, emotional responses and thinking patterns that generate my social results).
3. *There is no failure, just feedback* (all setbacks are opportunities for learning, and when I declare something as a failure, I close the feedback loop).
4. *When something is not working, do something different* (notice when a strategy is generating un-resourceful results and change the strategy).
5. *Mind and body are one system* (how I think will affect how I emote, which will affect how I behave).
6. *The meaning of your communication is the response you get* (it is the receiver of our intended messages that gives them meaning and how they respond indicates how they framed our intended message).
7. *Respect each other's maps of the world* (everyone will have their own point of view, and they have the right to hold this as long as it does not harm anyone).

The exercise could be facilitated via a team coaching process. One colleague coaches another through the reflexive process regarding each of the philosophical themes detailed above. The process involves coaching the person reflecting through surface-level reflection, mid-level reflection and deep-structure reflexivity to flesh out the elements that resonate with the participant and those that do not, specifically, what they identify as alternative leadership principles.

The meta-model

Another effective coaching tool for encouraging reflexivity in conscious leaders is the meta-model which is a language-based analytical tool developed by

Bandler and Grinder (1975). Largely due to the incredible amount of sense data, we experience our mind naturally:

1. Deletes information.
2. Generalises from experience.
3. Distorts experience.

This is usually represented when we engage in surface-level reflection. When one is trying to lead with conscious awareness, applications of deletion, generalisation and distortion of our experience and intended meanings can be significant barriers to establishing a generative dialogue with followers. This is because, as conscious leaders, we need a deeper understanding of the nature of our own and of others' sense-making structures so that we may obtain a richer perceptual map of the issues that are important to our teams. We need this to develop greater behavioural flexibility and emotional flexibility and to generate a transition from our closed perspective to open, differentiated and, ultimately, integrated perspectives that unite followers behind a leader's agenda (Dixon, 1998). Another issue with deletions, distortions and generalisations is the way that they can frame reality in such a way that supports a model 1 mindset (see Chapter 5) and discourages enquiry through dialogue.

Enabling reflexivity with the meta-model

When used carefully, the meta-model can trigger reflective thinking on the part of another. The meta-model, as a coaching tool, can "loosen the lid" on an individual's reality constructions and, essentially, enables reflexivity. The meta-model provides questions that function as sense-making catalysts to facilitate conscious leadership reflexivity. O'Connor and Seymour (2011, p. 92) describe the meta-model as consisting of: "A series of questions that seek to reverse and unravel the deletions and distortions and generalizations of language". By actively listening for "meta-model violations" – a term associated with Bandler and Grinder (1975) to describe linguistic statements containing either generalisations, distortions or deletions – and then asking questions to clarify and encourage re-evaluation, the conscious leader as a coach can skilfully lead themselves or a colleague through a process of self-realisation and thus build their capability in-terms of behavioral and emotional flexibility.

The main advantage of the meta-model as a sense making, or coaching tool is that it enables the analysis of surface level thinking to chunk down into the richer and more detailed aspects of the sense making experience. Meta- model violations as a construct enable this process. The basic elements of the meta-model are presented in Tables 14.1, 14.2 and 14.3:

Table 14.1 Meta-model Violations: Deletions

Meta-model Category	Example	Strategies for Exploring Distortions
Unspecified Noun	*"Everyone knows that you learn leadership from experience, not at college."*	*"Who specifically knows that?"*
Unspecified Verb	*"John has been really successful at leading his team."*	*"How specifically has John done that?"*
Comparison	*"This strategy is an important change leadership asset."*	*"Compared with what?"*
Judgement	*"There are people who just don't think the programme is making adequate progress."*	*"Who is making this judgement?"* *"On what grounds are they making this judgement?"*

Table 14.2 Meta-model Violations: Generalisations

Meta-model Category	Example	Strategies for Exploring Distortions
Modal Operator of Possibility	*"You can be whatever you want to be if you start to dream it and then have the will to become it."*	*"What would happen if you did?"* *"What would happen if you did not?"* *"What prevents you from . . . ?"*
Modal Operator of Necessity	*"Everything you do at work must be done to the very highest standard at all times."*	*"What would happen if you did?"* *"What would happen if you did not?"*
Universal Quantifier	*"I am the kind of person who never gets promoted."*	*"Has there ever been a time when . . .?"*

Table 14.3 Meta-model Violations: Distortions

Meta-model Category	Example	Strategies for Exploring Distortions
Complex Equivalent	*"He is not looking at me, so he is not listening to what I say."*	*"How does this mean that?"*
Presupposition	*"A lack of question from the audience means that they understand the main issues presented."*	*"What leads you to believe that?"*
Cause and Effect	*"Investing capital will generate profit."*	*"How exactly does this cause that? What would have to happen for this not to be caused by that?"*
Mind Reading	*"I can see that you think this is a bad idea."*	*"How exactly do you know that?"*

An exercise

If a change participant were asked to comment on how they thought the change programme they were part of was working, they could make the following statement:

It is a pity that they could not have sold the idea behind the change to us properly. After all, everyone knows that in the past, these things do not work. They are supposed to lead us, yet it is generally understood that they don't even bother to do this. They believe that all they need to do is command a change and change will happen. People will just fall into line. Well, it's not that simple; research tells us that communication and the buy-in of the people affected by the change are crucial if the change is to have any success. No wonder people lack commitment and don't take the change project seriously. The more they tell us what to do, the more we don't think about "how" best to do it; and that is a shame.

The above transcript appears quite detailed though it is, in fact, constituted by mainly surface-level reflections. It has examples of distortions, generalisations and deletions that one would associate with surface-level reflections. We invite you as the reader to identify the meta-model violations embedded in the text. Then select appropriate meta-model questions that you could use if you were coaching this person through a process of reflexivity. The meta-model, because of its usefulness for clarifying, challenging and stimulating new ways of thinking, is highly effective as a coaching tool to facilitate reflexivity in conscious leaders.

Reflexivity and personal development

Conscious leadership in practice involves the development of one's full potential to master one's emotional, cultural, behavioural, social and intellectual intelligences. Reflexivity has long been associated with learning (Schön, 1983). A fruitful source of personal development enabled through reflexivity is to examine our theory of action and compare this with our theory in action. For example, a leader may hold the theory of action that they are democratic leaders who advocate and encourage dialogue in their teams. This belief may be one that is central to their professional identity as a leader. They may judge others against this standard, and this judgement will more than likely influence the way the leader interacts with their colleague. The problem in these relationships, particularly between leaders and potential followers, arises when the theory in action, e.g., how the leader communicates, is incongruent with their theory of action. If, when communicating, the leader actually engages in monologue as a general communicative strategy and lacks disciplined listening skills, then we have a clear mismatch between their theory of action and their theory in action. This mismatch often occurs below conscious awareness. However, the mismatch, when consciously identified by followers, may provide a source of resentment and tensions in the leadership/membership dynamics.

Through coaching, either through one's internal coach or with the support of an external coach, the conscious leader can reflect on the social feedback they are receiving from their team members in terms of the strength of rapport. They may have identified that team members feel psychologically unsafe in relation to speaking up in their presence. By adopting the second and third perceptual position, which involves taking the perspective of team members and that of an objective outsider, they can engage in reflexivity regarding the mismatch between their theory of action and their theory in action regarding their communication habits. This process of deep reflexivity can awaken in the leader the realisation that they need to be the leader that they want to see in others; they must model the behaviours of participative democratic leadership. This means changing their communication strategies and habits. They need to model active listening skills and encourage free-flowing expression of thought in team members and resist the temptation to fall into extended monologues. This is generative change, i.e., bringing into the world a new version of themselves as a leader that is congruent with their theory of themselves in action. Such personal generative development based upon reflexivity can and should induce a change in the target of rapport between the leader and their team members.

Mindfulness and conscious leaders

Conscious leadership can be a challenging and stressful affair. It is important that the leader takes care of themselves in terms of their emotional, physical and intellectual health. Leaders are, after all, human beings, and if they become overloaded with stress, then they can burn out, lose their sense of vitality and, in some cases, even experience stress-related illness. Mindfulness is a highly effective self-management system for gauging and improving one's psychological, emotional and physical health. Mindfulness is defined by Baer (2003, p. 125) as follows: "Mindfulness involves intentionally bringing one's attention to the internal and external experiences occurring in the present moment and is often taught through a variety of meditation exercises". An important belief of conscious leadership is that body and mind are one system, and if any element of that system is unhealthy, this will affect the rest of the system negatively. Organisations such as Google, the Mayo Clinic, and the US Army use mindfulness training to improve workplace functioning, and the use of organisational mindfulness practices is increasing. Reflexivity can be accessed through simple mindfulness techniques such as the one we describe below.

Studies in multidisciplinary fields, such as behavioural science and organisational psychology, indicate strongly that mindfulness practices build resilience, improve mental and physical health and support people involved in challenging occupations in quite positive ways (Rupprecht et al., 2019).

Mindfulness aims to achieve an enhanced state of acute clarity of mind, focus and reflection to expand our awareness of our internal states, how our energy is influencing our behaviour and the attitudes and behaviours in others in the present moment. Mindfulness involves a process of quietening the mind to increase our internal and external awareness. Mindfulness also involves being sensitive to the energy we are giving off as a result of our emotional states. To quieten the mind may seem rather odd, and we invite you to try out the following mindfulness inducement exercise:

1. Find a moment where you can be alone and undisturbed.
2. Sit with the soles of your feet flat on the ground so you can feel the ground and close your eyes.
3. Imagine there is a length of string running through your spine and coming out of your head.
4. Imagine some force is gently pulling on that string to straighten your spine and posture.
5. Now focus on the number 100, see the number 100 in your mind's eye, hear it and see it.
6. Then start counting back from 100 to 0, maintaining an upright posture, eyes closed and allowing a slight pause between each number.

How did that feel? Did you notice that your mind started to quieten? Did you get past 70 without any struggle to pay attention? Did you feel relaxed and aware? The evidence suggests that simple mindful inducement techniques such as the one above can help us expand our awareness, elicit internally relaxed states and increase our attention levels. Learning mindfulness techniques is not too difficult. One can simply buy a mindfulness audiobook or an app and start building one's understanding of the practice and then, of course, practise its techniques. The evidence that indicates the value of mindfulness for developing one's conscious leadership skills is the quality of our own experience as mindfulness practitioners. As a conscious leader, mindfulness can help with the following activities detailed in Table 14.4:

Mindfulness techniques can also be practised as you work. For example, when you know you are to enter a team meeting, you can simply take a few minutes to calibrate your thoughts, emotions and energy and simply do the following mindful technique called "Ha breathing" (James, 2013), which is a Hawaiian Huna technique that is used to elicit a highly resourceful emotional, intellectual and behavioural state based upon mindfulness:

1. Pause, sit upright or stand straight, shoulders back and spine straightened.
2. Breathe in deeply through your nose for the count of three.
3. Exhale fully through your mouth, making a quiet "haaaaaaa" sound with your exhaled breath; stretch it as far as you can.
4. Pause, then repeat steps 2 and 3 five more times.

Table 14.4 Activities Supported by Mindfulness

Activity	Benefits of Mindfulness
Delivering a presentation.	Clears the mind and calms the nerves.
Handling a challenging meeting.	Elicits a gentle, non-judgemental presence.
Listening with attention.	Quietens the mind and enhances listening.
Calibrating an audience.	Expands one's peripheral vision and sense of awareness.
Managing energy levels.	Turns the attention and awareness inwards and calibrates energy levels, pacing these in terms of cognitive, emotional and behavioural activity levels by triggering a mindfulness technique.
Sleeping properly.	Simply count from 100 to 0 as previous to induce a highly relaxed state and peaceful mind.
Dealing with criticism.	Being mindful of how one reacts to criticism, reframing the meaning one attaches to it as constructive feedback, listening without judgement and looking for opportunities to learn from the feedback.

Mindfulness is one very productive and relatively straightforward body of applied practice that can expand our internal and external awareness and enable us to shift and reframe perspectives, alter our thought patterns, elicit positive emotional and behavioural states and manage our stamina and reliance. Mindfulness enables the acute focusing of our awareness regarding the present moment – whilst accepting it without judgment.

Conclusion

As human beings, we learn through experience, either directly or indirectly, to avoid the trap of functional stupidity (Alvesson and Spicer, 2016), which involves being discouraged by our culture to critically reflect upon our experiences. Unfortunately, examples of functional stupidity are commonplace. They are the result of an over-reliance on the model 1 mindset and the presence of a firmly established impoverished transactional leadership culture. The phenomenon of a mismatch between one's theory of action and one's theory in action is an example of the stupidity paradox as enshrined in folklore through the fable crafted by Hans Christian Anderson of the emperor who wore no clothes and yet believed he was wearing a robe made of beautiful materials that only those who were not stupid could see. Reflexivity, supported by mindfulness, is a conscious leadership competence that minimises the risk of functional stupidity in leaders; and one could argue that not investing in building a conscious leadership culture is, itself, an act of functional stupidity. In the next chapter, we shall review behavioural modelling as a conscious leadership practice.

References

Alvesson, M., Blom, M. & Sveningsson, S. (2017) *Reflexive Leadership: Organising in an Imperfect World*. Sage.

Alvesson, M. & Spicer, A. (2016) *The Stupidity Paradox: The Power and Pitfalls of Functional Stupidity at Work*. Profile Books.

Baer, A.R. (2003) Mindfulness Training as a Clinical Intervention: A Conceptual and Empirical Review. *Clinical Psychology Science and Practice*, 10(2).

Bandler, R. & Grinder, J. (1975) *Patterns of the Hypnotic Techniques of Milton H. Erickson, M.D.*, vol. 1. Meta Publications.

Dixon, N.M. (1998) *Dialogue at Work*. Lemos & Crane.

Greenwood, J. (1998) The Role of Reflection in Single and Double Loop Learning. *Journal of Advanced Nursing*, 27(5), pp. 1048–1053.

James, M. (2013) www.psychologytoday.com/gb/blog/focus-forgiveness/201303/increase-your-energy-in-three-minutes.

McGregor, D (1960) *The Human Side of Enterprise*. McGraw-Hill.

O'Connor, J. & Seymour, J. (2011) *Introducing NLP: Psychological Skills for Understanding and Influencing People*. HarperCollins.

Rupprecht, S., Falke, P., Kohls, N., Tamdjidi, C., Wittmann, M. & Kersemaekers, W. (2019) Mindful Leader Development: How Leaders Experience the Effects of Mindfulness Training on Leader Capabilities. *Frontiers in Psychology*, p. 1081.

Schön, D.A. (1983) *The Reflective Practitioner: How Professionals Think in Action*. Basic Books.

Tosey, P. & Mathison, J. (2009) *Neuro-Linguistic Programming: A Critical Appreciation for Managers and Developers*. Palgrave Macmillan.

15 MODELLING CONSCIOUS LEADERSHIP

Introduction

This chapter addresses what we believe is significant learning from the research we undertook to compose our book. The learning is best explored through a question which is framed as: *"How would an aspiring conscious leader learn the capabilities to emerge as a conscious leader?"* This question invites one's curiosity to learn about learning. Yes, reading a book like this will help you in this personal learning and development journey as you transition towards a practising conscious leader with the integrity of practice. However, you also need a learning strategy that is accessible, easy to understand, effective as a learning enabler and one that can be embedded into the culture of the organisation you represent as a conscious leader. The learning strategy that we feel best fits with the learning task, establishing a conscious leadership culture, is behavioural modelling (Dilts, 1998). This chapter chunks down and focuses in upon modelling conscious leadership moments, which are moments in time when a conscious leader demonstrates their conscious leadership competencies. We have decided to focus in on conscious leadership moments as they are small enough to generate rich analytical insights into the critical success factors that underpin a successful leadership moment. This chapter is concerned with introducing participants to the concept of behavioural modelling and, specifically, modelling conscious leadership.

Defining behavioural modelling

The process involved in behavioural modelling is based upon the theory that we all use strategies to generate our social results. These strategies can be identified and learned by others. Behavioural modelling has its roots in the pioneering work of behavioural change experts John Grinder and Richard Bandler, who, supported by their research teams, successfully modelled the success factors that enabled extraordinary success in therapy as delivered by world-class therapists such as Virginia Satir, Fritz Perls and Milton H. Erikson.

Behavioural modelling has been defined as follows: "Behaviour modelling involves observing and mapping the successful processes which underlie an

DOI: 10.4324/9781003272793-16

exceptional performance of some type" (Dilts, 1998, p. 29). Dilts continues with his explanation of behavioural modelling when he states that: "The purpose of behaviour modelling is to create a pragmatic map or 'model' of that behaviour which can be used to reproduce or stimulate some aspect of that performance by anyone who is motivated to do so. The goal of the behaviour modelling process is to identify the essential elements of thought and action required to produce the desired response or outcome". Behavioural modelling is not only analytical; it is also very experiential. Once a map of how a person creates their social results has been composed, the next step is for the modeller to start inculcating the beliefs and values that drive the expressive strategies of the modelling subject. They must become the change they want to see in themselves and in others. The operating principles of behavioural modelling are cited by Potter (2018, p. 45 inspired by the work of Dilts, (1998)) as follows:

- All excellent behaviour can be considered as a *"social strategy"*.
- Social strategies can be *"process mapped"*.
- Each element of the strategic process can be *"modelled"*.
- Social strategies, once process mapped, are known as *"patterns"*.
- We can *"imprint"* ourselves into the psychology of the performer we wish to model.
- We can focus on *"what"* the performer does and *"how"* and *"why"* they do it.
- We can isolate the *"discreet parts"* of the pattern for study and understanding.
- We can *"delete parts"* that do not have much influence on the outcome.
- Thus, we can *"re-engineer"* a pattern for accelerated learning.
- We can design *"teaching strategies"* so that others can learn the pattern.

The power of modelling is that one's modelling capabilities are greatly enhanced when one becomes unconsciously competent at the modelling process through study at a conscious level of the modelling processes. Reflective practice makes perfect practice. Essentially, behavioural modelling is a learning strategy operated with a high level of conscious awareness that aims to identify the key success factors that are the difference that makes the difference in successful performers and install these in others to achieve similar results as the modelling subject (Dilts, 1998). Behavioural modelling is especially effective when the unit of analysis is clearly circumscribed and chunked down to a manageable level of operational detail, such as leadership moments rather than leadership as a general process.

Modelling conscious leadership moments

A leadership moment is any moment in time where a line manager shifts their identity into that of a conscious leader. For example, if we consider, as a leadership moment, an executive manager who is excellent at delivering presentations with conscious awareness, someone who seems very calm although enthusiastic and who appears to bring presence to the role and positively engages with their audience, behavioural modelling would aim to unpack the strategies that this manager employs to generate these states. Behavioural modelling is a method we use to unpack the critical success factors that underpin successful outcomes and then teach others how to install these. Thus, we can use behavioural modelling techniques as analytical tools to unpack and map out the traits that sustain a model of leadership in a significant other.

Once the modelling map of the leadership moment, e.g., delivering a presentation with conscious awareness, is complete to a level of pragmatic utility, then the next step involves developing training programmes based on modelling principles informed by the modelling map to inculcate a management community regarding the conscious change leadership model we are advancing, e.g., how to present with conscious awareness. The techniques that one would use to install the success factors mapped from the modelling process can be sourced from the fields of life/leadership coaching, mentoring, acting and mindfulness. It is also important when transitioning from an impoverished transactional leadership culture to an enriching transactional leadership culture enabled by conscious leadership practices that the modelling process is supported by active coaches/mentors who would support participants throughout their journey and model in themselves the valued success factors that generate the desired leadership outcomes.

How does behavioural modelling work?

Behavioural modelling works because it is based on the principles that enable the successful production and reproduction of culture. Behavioural modelling is not always done at a conscious level. We are all culturally wired to unconsciously model excellent social strategies demonstrated by significant others in our experiences (Bourdieu, 1991). In all ethnic cultures, local members intuitively and consciously model the cultural norms of their peers, such as the local language, behaviours, emotions, ethics and standards of dress. This intuitive modelling process clearly happens below conscious awareness; however, it is supported by conscious modelling processes such as formal instruction from parents and significant others and educational programmes. What behavioural modelling does is provide a qualitative research strategy through which the "modeller" can create a distilled map of the critical success factors that underpin the model that people use to achieve an outcome. Bearing in mind that the purpose of culture is to gain control over one's environment so that the group may be successful, then it is logical to assume that if a leadership style is seen to be successful, others will unconsciously model the success factors that generate the leadership style and its social results.

We need only glance at the myriad of ethnic, corporate and regional cultures throughout the world to see overwhelming evidence of behavioural modelling at work. Modelling is the cultural glue that holds the shared identities of cultural groups together. Modelling is a social constructive process and as stated previously can operate both intuitively and consciously. The ability to gain social acceptance as a leader is to a large degree influenced by ones ability to model the cultural norms of the group one is wishing to lead.

Emerging leaders are influenced unconsciously by the leadership style of their active role models throughout the organisation. The human brain appears to be culturally sensitive to selecting and internalising the habits, behaviours, values and beliefs of significant others throughout its social environment. This capability is an essential survival mechanism as it is required to ensure acceptance within the group and thus benefit from its protection and opportunities for growth and development. Language as a modelled construct is an excellent example of unconscious modelling if this is the native language of the speaker.

Modelling conscious leadership moments in practice

This section will provide a brief review of some of the typical stages involved in a behavioural modelling project based upon the work of Robert Dilts (1998). As stated previous, behavioural modelling of conscious leadership moments involves identifying the success factors that underpin a successful performance on the part of a role model. This is fundamentally a research project. This modelling research process is explained in more detail below.

Behavioural modelling research methods

Essentially, behavioural modellers are researchers; they are curious people who look, listen and feel for data concerning the success factors that a role model employs to achieve a successful outcome. This process would be driven by the question, *"How would you identify the key success factors that your role model uses to generate their leadership moment successfully over time?"* Table 15.1 lists a range of research methods that can be used as effective tools to conduct an analytical modelling exercise.

Deep structure interview

A fundamental modelling research method is the "deep structure interview", which involves two stages. Stage 1 involves arranging to meet with the modelling subject to understand, from their perspective, what the criteria for presenting successfully with conscious awareness would be. As with all modelling projects, it is essential that the modellers can envisage what success looks like, sounds like and even feels like. Thus, being able to pinpoint performance indicators which signify excellent achievement of a leadership moment, such as presenting with conscious awareness, is crucial. The method we adopt to do

Table 15.1 Modelling Research Methods

Research Method	Description
Shadowing	This involves simply following your role model and observing what they do.
Participant observation	This involves attending a specific event where the role model performs their task and the participant observer simply observes.
360-degree feedback	This involves gauging feedback from people who report to your role model regarding the leadership moment.
Re-enactment	This involves inviting the subject to think of a time when they delivered an effective presentation and re-enact it for the modeller.
Role play	This involves inviting the subject to co-deliver a simulated presentation with the modeller, possibly including a role-playing audience.
Beliefs audit	This involves exploring with the subject the main beliefs that they hold about the leadership moment, e.g., delivering a successful presentation.
Values audit	This involves exploring with the subject the main values that they consider important about the leadership moment.
Deep structure interview	This is a semi-structured interview during which the modeller interviews the subject to enable deep structure exploration regarding their leadership moment.
Domain analysis	This involves identifying categories of meaning the role model uses to structure their experience, e.g., focusing in upon one's breathing as a kind of relaxation technique.
Theme analysis	This is a type of analysis that seeks to identify patterns of success factors that emerge as recurring themes from the multiple data sources.
Causal maps analysis	This is a type of analysis that aims to identify causation between variables. For example, the subject may believe that cleansing their hands generates a clean and untroubled mind.
Triple description	This involves gaining three alternative perspectives regarding a situation: • First Position: That of the modeller. • Second position: That of the role model. • Third position: That of the objective observer.

this is to create a criterion of excellence which serves to profile what success looks, sounds and feels like regarding a specific leadership moment.

Stage 2 of the modelling process is to, once again, arrange to interview the modelling subject to follow up on the initial deep structure interview. This time, we would be interested in "how" they generate the successful outcomes that they associated with a successful team meeting from the first deep structure interview detailed above. A modelling strategy worksheet (Dilts, 1998) is a useful tool to help guide this stage in the modelling process. We would create a modelling strategy worksheet for each sensory category of evidence.

Participant observation

The next stage is to participate in the modelling subject's actual presentation and to observe the use of the visible strategies they employ and the assumed effects that they generate. In this event, the modelling researcher could take notes of the tonal marking, body language and linguistic patterns adopted by the modelling subject. These notes could then be used to either clear up some ambiguity with the modelling subject post-presentation and/or be used to validate their beliefs regarding the strategies they employ and their effects. The final stage, thereafter, in the analytical research process is to produce the report of the strategies the modeller employs called a modelling map and ask them to read it through and confirm that it meets with their understanding of what they do.

Role play

This stage involves the modeller adopting the content of the modelling map in a role play situation. The modeller, along with some other managers who are to model the modelling subject's strategy, meet with the role model and an independent observer and simulate an actual presentation. The role model is directed by the modeller to enact specific chunks of an actual presentation. The modelling team, who would have studied the modelling map, observe the role model throughout the enacting. Then, in turns, each participant takes the floor from the role model and adopts their strategies and enacts the specific stage of the presentation. They then get constructive feedback from the actual role model and the modelling team as well as the other participants.

Mentoring

The last stage in this process involves assigning a mentor to the conscious leaders who are in transition and are modelling the new behaviours, values and beliefs. This is either the original role model or another role model who has been identified as exemplifying the model that is being advanced throughout the leadership culture as the archetypical model that is to be valued as a leadership moment regarding presenting. The mentor meets with the mentee and discusses the model and their feelings regarding this. They identify with the mentee any challenges or limiting beliefs that may be blocking their ability to fully embrace the model as their model. Then, they join the mentee as they deliver presentations and sponsor their adoption of the new model and give constructive feedback post-presentation.

360-Degree feedback

It is vital that the OD modelling team establish the perspective of team members who experience presentations before the modelling exercise is started. This, ideally, involves a process of feedback regarding the presenters' states when presenting and the effects on team members' dynamics. Then, once the modelling project has been completed with the team leader having been invited to adopt the model in the context of presenting, further feedback research is conducted to help evaluate the impact on team dynamics that can be associated with the new strategies being modelled by the role model. This feedback is then shared with the modeller by their mentor, and, if required, further modelling support via coaching and mentoring is provided.

Conclusion

A significant learning that we wish to share with you is that the above process is detailed, lengthy and time-consuming. However, the effort involved in transitioning from an impoverished transactional leadership culture to one that is enriching and facilitated by conscious leadership practices is equally complex and exhausting. There are no shortcuts or quick wins. Creating a conscious leadership culture is a long-term project. It must be based upon valid research findings, which is the hallmark of action research and the OD movement. Organisational development should aim to ensure that all managers are trained as coach mentors and are competent in aspects of business and lifestyle coaching and mentoring techniques. The process documented above should be internalised as a core cultural value that is inextricably linked to the normative skill set of the line manager. In Robert Dilts' (2003) terms: the manager must also be a coach, a leader, an awakener, a guide, a mentor and a caretaker of a psychologically safe workspace. This multi-dimensional corporate identity insists that OD should not be marginalised and that conscious leadership training is not assigned to a two-day course every 12 or 18 months; rather, it should be integrated into the cultural fabric of the organisation, and this takes leadership . . . or, specifically, conscious leadership. Our final chapter will consider the strategic approach leaders could adopt to establishing a conscious leadership culture.

References

Bourdieu, P. (1991) *Language and Symbolic Capital*. Polity Press.

Dilts, R. (1998) *Modelling with NLP*. Meta Publications.

Dilts, R. (2003) *From Coach to Awakener*. Meta Publications.

Potter, D. (2018) *Neuro-Linguistic Programming for Change Leaders: The Butterfly Effect*. Routledge.

16 BUILDING A CULTURE OF CONSCIOUS LEADERSHIP

Introduction

Our final chapter pulls on key themes that underpin elements of the preceding chapters to provide an outline strategy regards how one approaches the task of building a conscious leadership culture. We start with the task of framing organisational culture and then defining cultural change work. The idea that stakeholder engagement and leadership capabilities should be embedded into the corporate governance of the organisation and risk assessed yearly is then introduced. We examine the process of awakening the need for change in leadership styles. The role of dialogue seminars as key technology to support the case for change is emphasised once more. We then revisit coaching as an enabler for cultural change and survey some examples of training approaches that could aid the development of conscious leadership competencies. We conclude with the argument that the potential success of this cultural change process is dependent on the active and present role modelling of a conscious leadership mindset throughout the leadership network within an organisation.

Framing organisational culture and cultural change

When defining culture, Park (1950, p. 3) claims that: "We may say that culture consists of those habits in individuals that have become customary, conventionalized, and accepted in the community". Culture is both a process of sense-making and a system of control that originates from the sense-making process (McCalman and Potter, 2015). The beliefs that are generated through group sense-making generate core values that function to control expressive group choices. For example, a management team, over time, may construct a shared belief that leadership is something that is learned through practical experience; it is not something you learn from books. This belief may generate a core value that such an organisation values practical experience over formal study. This is arguably a limiting belief. The cultural change project, in this case, might involve targeting such a core belief and related values to change these. The desired change may involve introducing a new belief, one that values both practical leadership development supported by a formal study on leadership programmes.

DOI: 10.4324/9781003272793-17

Schein (2004, p. 17) defines culture as: "A basic pattern of shared basic assumptions that was learnt by a group as it solved its problems of external adaptation and internal integration, that has worked well enough to be considered valid, and, therefore, to be taught to new members as the correct way to perceive, think and feel in relation to those problems". This definition points towards the shared nature of organisational culture and its functional and practical purpose, which is to allow cultural members to benefit from the control and management of their environment. This fact indicates the challenge involved in changing culture as the cultural norms of a group of managers may have served them well over time and helped them develop and even prosper. They may be defended with vigour. Thus the case for change and the need for dialogue to help unfreeze cultural attitudes and, subsequently, restructure these for inculcation and then to re-freeze as the new culture is critical (Lewin, 1951).

McCalman and Potter (2015, p. 19) define organisational cultural change as: "A fundamental change in the meanings that cultural members attribute to their values and assumptions, which leads to a shift in the nature of cultural themes in use and the expressive content of the cultural paradigm". Alvesson and Sveningsson (2008, p. 42) put forward a related description of cultural change work as follows: "A cultural change is not that management tries to impose new behaviours (or talk), but a change of the ideas, values and meanings of large groups of people". It is clear from the above that the unit of analysis when attempting cultural change comprises beliefs, values and the related behaviours of a cultural group. Thus, attempting to change a leadership style in a management team would constitute a cultural change project as the leadership style that is established will be based upon highly entrenched beliefs and values shared within the management team.

Corporate governance and auditing leadership culture

A current issue that is highly prominent within the business world is the practice of corporate governance, which can be defined as follows: "Corporate governance deals with the ways in which suppliers of finance to corporations assure themselves of getting a return on their investment" (Schleifer and Vishny, 1997, p. 1). Corporate governance aims to mitigate the risk of stakeholders not receiving the full value from their investment in the organisation. By stakeholders, we mean any individual or group who has an investment in the ongoing success of the organisation regardless of whether the investment is economical, social, cultural or emotional.

It may be the case, as we have discussed, that a leadership culture is historically based upon an emphasis of profit purely defined in economic terms, operating without conscious leadership awareness and from a model 1 mindset. We can imagine such an organisation being faced with change drivers in society to adopt a greater sense of corporate responsibility and govern their corporate affairs with an enhanced state of awareness regarding the impact their leaders' decisions have on all stakeholders. The device that could enable this awakening process and the associated change in mindset from a transactional leadership culture to a conscious leadership culture rooted in a model 2 leadership mindset could be the corporate governance framework adopted by the organisation.

Essentially, corporate governance aims to minimise risk. It can be used to recognise the relationship between the quality of the organisation's leadership and the ability to operate as a sustainable business that is both fit for purpose in the present and in the future. This means that we have a potentially highly potent tool for triggering reflexivity regarding the leadership culture of an organisation.

As leadership is so important, especially with regard to strategy development, then the quality and suitability of the leadership culture in use should be evaluated at regular intervals in terms of its risk impact on current and future trading and strategic operations. Essentially, just as the quality, technological and economic systems are risk assessed as a standard throughout industry, the leadership culture should be equally valued as a target for risk assessment, and this value should come from a shared belief within the board of directors that leadership has a profound impact on corporate sustainability. The board would consider, as part of its governance strategies, the following risk assessment techniques, which, taken together, constitute a cultural audit to identify the nature and effectiveness of the leadership style within the leadership group:

1. 360-degree feedback.
2. Staff engagement assessment survey.
3. Stakeholder focus groups.
4. One-to-one leadership interviews.
5. Leadership assessment centres.
6. Analysis of strategic change drivers.

This risk assessment framework as a cultural audit would be used to generate valid data to:

- Evaluate the distance between a model 1 and a model 2 mindset.
- Establish the weighting of the existing leadership culture in relation to conscious leadership practices.
- Assess the suitability of the existing leadership culture to support immediate trading needs and implement strategy.
- Assess the ability of the established leadership culture to concentrate both on immediate operational concerns and strategic concerns aimed at creating a sustainable business fit for the future.
- Identify change drivers that are shaping the present and the future.
- Identify behaviours, capabilities, values and beliefs that are required to maximise the immediate potential and the future potential of the organisation.
- Evaluate the strength of stakeholder engagement with the organisational leadership.
- Assess the strength of connection that the leaders and their stakeholders have with the vision, mission, purpose and ambitions of the organisation.

The data generated from the risk assessment framework regarding leadership culture can then be used to inform the ongoing personal development of the organisation's leaders in line with a competency framework that supports the current and future needs of the organisation. This awakening process would be driven by the corporate governance framework with high profile executive leadership at the board level. Corporate governance can and should be used to drive the awakening process by identifying the nature of a leadership culture as a potential risk to the sustainability of the organisation.

The Butterfly Effect; a metaphor for incremental cultural change work

Once the focus of change and the case for change have both been established, then the wicked problem (Grint, 2008) of actually attempting cultural change is to be addressed. Assuming the cultural change problem is to shift an impoverished transactional leadership culture towards an enriching model that is enabled through conscious leadership practices, then a strategy for change is required. Bearing in mind that cultural change involves changing specific beliefs and values to generate new strategies for behaving, thinking and emoting (McCalman and Potter, 2015), any cultural change strategy must always have, at its centre, social interaction and sense-making.

Leaders need a simple yet convincing model of change that they can engage with quickly and effectively. They also need to feel that they can affect the changes and, therefore, have control over the change process. Thus, if the leaders themselves become their own personal change project and are open to conscious leadership personal development techniques, then they can stimulate the butterfly effect throughout their organisation to generate systematic and incremental cultural changes in the established leadership styles. They can own their own change project, which is themselves, and, thus, they decide the degree of commitment they are prepared to give to such a change project. The butterfly effect can be interpreted as a metaphor for initiating incremental cultural change through an emergent influential leader consciously changing aspects of their leadership style (Potter, 2018).

The basic principle of the butterfly effect as a theory of cultural change is that if a leader, as a significant other, models habitually new behavioural, emotional and cognitive strategies, these will be intuitively and consciously modelled by their peers and the team leaders who are in their in-group. Those team leaders who are in the senior leaders' out-group will also experience different relationships with these leaders who are actively modelling the new conscious leadership practices that may lead to higher levels of rapport between both leaders and followers. Thus, out-group members have the opportunity to merge into in-group members through modelling the new leadership style. Both parties, leaders and team members, will experience a more enjoyable and rewarding experience of work and be far more open to aligning themselves positively behind the vision, mission and ambitions of the organisation at large (Omilion-Hodges and Ptacek, 2021).

The role of coaching and dialogue seminars is important when the process of awakening the desire to change one's beliefs and values and related leadership style is underway. Ideally, once valid information has been gathered via the yearly leadership cultural audit, it should be shared with the leadership team through a programme of dialogue seminars facilitated by conscious leadership coaches.

However, a prickly pear has to be managed sensitively before the dialogue seminars take place by the conscious leadership coaches. The premise that leaders express themselves the same way with all of their team members and, thus, their team members experience the same relations with their leaders is now a premise that would arguably lack credibility. The quality of LMX relationships will operate along a continuum of very weak to very strong rapport. Our model of anti-conscious leadership, introduced in Chapter 7, explains the dynamics of the social process that can lead to out-groups whose members will experience a very impoverished relationship with a leader. The conscious leadership coach should share a summary of the information from the leadership cultural audit with each member of the leadership team, especially the data generated from the 360-degree feedback process, involving all members of a leadership membership exchange group. The coaching process needs to also emphasise reflexivity on the part of the leader, who is the focus of the coaching process. The aim is to enable the leader to shift from their closed perspective to an open perspective (Dixon, 1998) before they join the dialogue seminars. The 360-degree feedback may clearly identify an in- and an out-group whose members experience varying degrees of rapport and, thus, influence with their leader. The nature of each relationship underpinning the dyads in both the in-group and the out-group would need to be reflected upon, and the associated beliefs that drive the nature of these relationships explored. This, of course, demands reflexivity and emotional intelligence on the part of the emergent conscious leader.

It is quite possible that a leader with a clear in-group may still generate significant qualities of our anti-conscious leadership model as part of the in-group LMX culture. A leader may also habitualise many of the elements of our anti-conscious leadership model presented in Chapter 7, with the exception of social rapport. Perhaps, if the leader and their in-group members have very similar demographic characteristics and share a career history, they may socialise together, share gossip and form political cabals. This degree of serious matching can generate a form of corporate hegemony and group think that insulates this elite group from others and maintains very distinct out-groups whose members may share very little in common with in-group members and their leader. Thus excessive corrective transactions may be understated within in-groups, and the relationships may border, if not fully occupy, the status of friendships. Psychological safety may still be low due to the leader and the in-group members' need for political alliances to maintain their privileges and influence. The leaders' influence may be strongly routed in ongoing rewards of some kind or another to in-group members. The individual leadership style as presented to their own leadership/membership exchange networks is likely to be impoverished and generative of CRASH state rather than COACH states throughout the leadership/membership exchange network groups.

One can quickly assume that trying to transform such leadership/membership exchange dynamics is a complex and challenging project. A significant barrier, as we have previously discussed, is a lack of leadership reflexivity characteristic of our anti-conscious leadership model. It is within the dialogue seminars that these leaders will be encouraged to hold multiple perspectives regarding the quality of leadership/membership exchange rapport with an open mind, and this is required to gradually move towards differentiated and, ultimately, a new group integrated perspective regarding the current utility of the established leadership style and its need for development based on the data generated from the leadership cultural audit.

Coaching reflexivity

Central to cultural change in leadership styles is reflexivity which we discussed throughout Chapter 14. The conscious leadership coach needs to support the leader to practise reflexive skills. A model that was discussed in Chapter 10 that can enable reflexive thinking is that of the four strategies for perspective-taking (Dixon, 1998). This model enables the coach to guide the client through an introspective process of discovery regarding their beliefs and the foundations of these beliefs that underpin LMX relationships in both the in-group and their out-group members.

Throughout the coaching session, the coach guides the client through Dixon's (1998) four stages of perspective-taking. From the initially closed perspective to an open perspective, to one where the client could differentiate between perspectives, to the final stage where they are open to the possibility of a dialogue with their team member and generating an integrated perspective together as a basis for moving forwards with their working relationship. If we assume that a leader has a member of their team who is an out-group member, the coaching dialogue may typically involve the following exchanges:

Coach: "What is your perspective regarding your relationship with David?"

Leader: "Mm . . . I think David is good at parts of his job though he can be quite confrontational and challenging. He is quite opinionated and does not really fit in with the team".

Coach: "I see . . . So this is your perspective . . . do you think we could stretch that a little to widen your perspective and perhaps open it up?"

Leader: "Okay, let's do that".

Coach: "What do you have in common with David?"

Leader: "Well, we both want to deliver high-quality services to our customers".

Coach: "Good . . . so you do have a shared core value then?"

Leader: "Yes, I guess, on reflection, we do".

Coach: "If you were to step into David's shoes and he is trying to generate excellence in service delivery, and perhaps some team members were not meeting his expectations, how would you feel about that?"

Leader: "Good question . . . I would feel frustrated and probably concerned".

Coach: "Is that how David would be feeling?"

Leader: "Yes, I think it would be".

Coach: "So that's something else you both have in common?"

Leader: "Yes, it is; I have never really thought about it that way".

Coach: "So you can see things from David's perspective then?"

Leader: "On this subject, yes . . . though it is the way he handles these situations I feel uneasy about".

Coach: "What is it about his handling of these challenges you feel uneasy about?"

Leader: "Well . . . I would adopt a less aggressive approach than David. I would discuss my concerns with the team members and address these that way".

Coach: "Have you asked David why he has not done that?"

Leader: "Mm . . . no, I have not".

Coach: "Why not?"

Leader: "Because I believe he would get defensive, and so I just maintain a social distance from him. It's easier".

Coach: "What is the basis of that belief for you?"

Leader: "Well . . . it's just my opinion based on what others have told me and how he reacts to being challenged at times in the management team".

Coach: "So you value harmony?"

Leader: "Yes".

Coach: "What would happen if you took David for lunch and explained your concerns and invited him to be open with you and share his feeling with you regards your concerns?"

Leader: "I do not know . . . I would worry that things got heated".

Coach: "So what will happen if you do not open up with David?"

Leader: "Things will remain the same".

Coach: "So David will remain in your out-group . . . you both will have weak rapport and little trust and effectively a fragile working relationship?"

> *Leader*: "Well, that is not an option? So I will reach out to David, and I will make every effort to understand his perspectives, and perhaps we can reach some sort of position that allows us to work closer together with greater rapport".

Model the leadership style you want to establish

The idea of modelling socially desirable beliefs and values expressed through behaviours, emotions and cognitive styles is firmly established within anthropology (Bourdieu, 1991), personal development (Dilts, 1998) and social learning theory (Bandura, 1977) and sociology (Blumer, 1969). Modelling, which we addressed in depth within Chapter 15, suggests that those in positions of influence, such as emergent leaders, should model the behaviours they want to encourage their followers to adopt. If an organisation looks towards encouraging its members to use specific behavioural, emotional and cognitive strategies as part of their LMX intra- and interpersonal dynamics, then these ideal states must start with and be routinely demonstrated authentically by those in titled leadership positions (Omilion-Hodges and Ptacek, 2021). This simple yet compelling principle, "to be the change you want to see in the world", drives cultural change work.

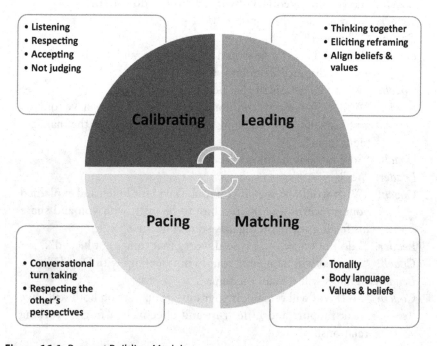

Figure 16.1 Rapport Building Model

Organisational culture is based upon social interactions rooted in beliefs and values. Therefore, cultural change must start with the individual, then the dyad, then the group and then the inter-group. LMX theory provides us with a superb complementary set of ideas through which to manoeuvre cultural change work. The question is, to change the nature of LMX cultural norms, where does one start? The rapport building model (O'Connor, & Seymour, 2011) is an excellent base to launch a cultural change project aimed towards establishing an enriching transactional or transformational leadership culture based upon conscious self-leadership practices.

Rapport building

We reviewed the rapport model in Chapter 7 (see Figure 16.1). Suffice to say that the continuum of quality of LMX relationships will be characterised by the quality of rapport between leaders and members. Therefore, understanding the elements of the rapport building model and using these as a coaching instrument, both in analytical terms and in interactive terms, would be central to building a culture of conscious leadership.

A simple questionnaire could be used to establish the perspectives between the leader and a specific team member who form a dyad regardless of whether the member is an in- or an out-group member (see Table 16.1).

Leadership questionnaire

Please reflect on each question below and allocate a grading regarding the quality of the relationship/behavioural traits you experience in your relationship with your leader or team member. The scale is 1 through to 5, with 1 signifying a very low score and 5 a very high score.

The distribution of ratings provides a reasonable indication regarding strengths that contribute towards establishing rapport and weaknesses that limit the potential of very deep rapport between leaders and team members. They also provide a basis for deep structure reflexivity regarding the ratings on the part of both the respondent and the focus of their ratings: their colleague.

Table 16.1 Leadership Questionnaire

Question	1	2	3	4	5
Calibrating					
How would you rate the quality of your colleague's ability to accurately read your state of mind?					
How would you rate the quality of your colleague's ability to pay attention to your thoughts and feelings?					

(Continued)

Table 16.1 Continued

Question	1	2	3	4	5
How would you rate the quality of your colleague's ability to read situations that you are involved in objectively?					
Pacing					
How would you rate the quality of your colleague's ability to patiently take time to understand your perspective?					
How would you rate the quality of your colleague's ability to be fully present when meeting with you?					
When you feel emotionally connected to a perspective, how would you rate the quality of your colleague's ability to empathise with you?					
Matching					
How would you rate the degree of similarity between you and your colleague regarding your approach to your work-based challenges?					
How would you rate the quality of your colleague's ability to accept and agree with your point of view?					
How would you rate the quality of your colleague's ability to accommodate and support your approach to work-based decisions?					
Leading					
How connected do you feel to your colleague's leadership style?					
How would you rate the quality of your colleague's ability to consider your feelings and needs as a team member? Leadership?					

Conclusion

Conscious leadership is, as Anderson and Anderson (2010) insightfully claim: "a way of being"; it is a model of human behaviour that looks inwardly and outwardly for practical resources to help the self be a far more flexible and resourceful leader. The key to building a culture based on conscious leadership principles is for significant leaders to authentically model these in their everyday interactions with team members. Omilion-Hodges and Ptacek (2021, p. 206) state that: "Leaders should always focus on the collective functioning of the group. They can do this by being mindful of the relationships they share with individual members, their resource distribution practices, and remaining aware of how their relationships and distribution of resources are perceived by the group". Their views are based on an extensive review of LMX literature spanning 20 years. Their views also confirm common sense anecdotal views of leaders and team members based on personal experience. However, there is a tendency, in the West especially, to emphasise hard skills in leaders such as planning, organising and analysing and to downplay soft intra- and interpersonal skills. Introducing conscious leadership practices to establish an enriching leadership culture that could graduate to embedding core transformational change competencies is not easy. However, with an open perspective based upon a growth mindset and operating from a field of shared psychological safety, establishing such an empowering and rewarding conscious leadership culture is entirely possible. The business case for investing in conscious leadership development is clear and compelling.

References

Alvesson, M. & Sveningsson, S. (2008) *Changing Organizational Culture: Cultural Change Work in Progress*. Routledge.

Anderson, D. & Anderson, L. (2010) *Beyond Change Management: How to Achieve Breakthrough Results Through Conscious Change Leadership*. John Wiley and Sons.

Bandura, A. (1977) Self-Efficacy: Toward a Unifying Theory of Behavioral Change. *Psychological Review*, 84(2), pp. 191–215.

Blumer, H. (1969) *Symbolic Interactionism*. University of California Press.

Bourdieu, P. (1991) *Language and Symbolic Capital*. Polity Press.

Dilts, R. (1998) *Modelling with NLP*. Meta Publications.

Dixon, N.M. (1998) *Dialogue at Work*. Lemos & Crane.

Grint, K. (2008) Wicked Problems and Clumsy Solutions: The Role of Leadership. *Clinical Leader*, 1(11).

Lewin, K. (1951) *Field Theory in Social Science*. Harper and Row.

McCalman, J. & Potter, D. (2015) *Leading Cultural Change: The Theory and Practice of Successful Organizational Transformation*. Kogan Page.

O'Connor, J. & Seymour, J. (2011) *Introducing NLP: Psychological Skills for Understanding and Influencing People*. HarperCollins.

Omilion-Hodges, L. & Ptacek, J. (2021) *What Is the Leader – Member Exchange (LMX) Theory?* Palgrave Macmillan.

Park, E.R. (1950) *Race and Culture*. The Free Press of Glencoe.

Potter, D. (2018) *Neuro-Linguistic Programming for Change Leaders: The Butterfly Effect*. Routledge.

Schein, E.H. (2004) *Organizational Culture and Leadership*, 3rd edn. Jossey-Bass.

Schleifer, A. & Vishny, W.R. (1997) A Study of Corporate Governance. *The Journal of Finance*, LII(2).

AFTERWORD

Leadership is not easy. Leadership as a social and cultural process is a complex affair fraught with many different challenges. Our book has not set out to make the act of leadership appear easy or to oversimplify the subject. What we have aimed to do is to present a set of ideas and methods that, with a little effort, can be understood and put into practice by anyone who is expected to fulfil a leadership function. The ideas and methods we have surveyed throughout this book simply need two critical qualities for the practitioner, that is: (1) to be prepared to adopt an open perspective; and (2) to engage in reflexivity. The well-known proverb; *"You can lead a horse to water, but you cannot make it drink"*. is useful to remind us of the fact that if potential leaders elect to maintain a closed perspective to developing their leadership potential and block any opportunities for reflexivity, then they will damage the potential of the leadership group to flourish. Potential leaders must want to learn how to become more productive and effective leaders; they cannot be made to learn.

Being closed to reflexive practice and adopting a closed perspective are hallmarks of a fixed mindset. The conundrum we must tackle in such cases is why do apparently smart people with responsibilities to their stakeholders to enable the growth and prosperity of the organisation adopt such counterintuitive strategies? If they were asked this question, it is likely that they would, in many cases, be offended and slip into immediate denial. This is because admitting to the habitual reliance on a closed perspective and resisting any reflexivity would not be compatible with their theory of self in action as a leader. Yet, in practice, often, potential leaders do refrain from reflexive practice, and they do hold onto and defend their closed perspectives. They essentially adopt the model 1 mindset.

It is still of great surprise when one meets a senior manager, who is considering some kind of organisational development intervention into their organisational culture, who refuses to try to explore multiple perspectives regarding how to think about and work with culture. They assume that they know what organisational culture is and how to "fix" it. Yet, when we introduce them to the principle of researching beliefs and values that drive expressions in their management teams, they look at us blankly. They simply don't know what they don't know that they don't know. They are often operating from a position of unconscious incompetence, and as they will not move from closed to open perspective-taking, supported by reflexive practice at individual and group levels, they cannot graduate through the learning process to a state of conscious competence or even unconscious mastery of their subject as leaders.

We were reminded of a situation where a consultant was working with a leadership team of ten executives. The issue at hand was a perception of staff disengagement throughout the business with the mission, vision and ambitions of the organisation. The ten leaders had "led" their teams for an average minimum of ten years. The consultant met with each individual executive and asked them to identify the cause of the disengagement. The executives poured out with enthusiasm the many reasons that were causing staff disengagement. Then the consultant invited all ten executives to a meeting to discuss their points of view, ensuring individual confidentially. The alleged "causes" were posted on flip chart sheets and spread around the conference room walls. The consultant then asked the executives to go around the room and study the alleged causes. Then, once they had settled around a conference table, the consultant went around the table clockwise, asking each executive the same questions:

1. "Do you feel that the alleged causes of staff disengagement posted around this room are credible and therefore legitimate?"

Without exception, each executive stated in reply that yes, they do feel that they were credible and thus legitimate. Then the consultant asked the second question of each executive one by one:

2. "What contribution do you make to either generating these causes or sustaining them?"

Each executive looked either tense, nervous or defensive, and some were even puzzled and irritated. Without exception, they did not recognise in any way that they, as individual leaders, had contributed to causing the disengagement catalysts or even sustaining them. The consultant then asked a third question, this time to the group:

3. "What has to change regarding your leadership for these disengagement catalysts to be removed?"

This question was a game-changer for this group of executives. It was an awakener. It stimulated intense group discussion and the realisation that staff disengagement does not occur in a vacuum. Whilst all staff do have some self-responsibility for their attitudes of choice, their leaders also have to perceive their disengagement as resistance to their leadership efforts, and in conscious leadership terms, resistance is a symptom of weak rapport. The executive team then agreed to work on their rapport building skills regarding their direct reports and their own peer relationships. This was the start of their conscious leadership journey.

So, the awakening process is the only antidote to an anti-conscious leadership mindset. The leadership team has to want to learn how to grow and develop as leaders. They must be prepared to acknowledge their responsibilities as leaders for crafting a climate of psychological safety to enable organisational learning at the level of the individual, the dyad, the group and the inter-group to flourish. This involves the role modelling of a growth mindset and model 2 leadership attitude. It involves mastering the basic principles of rapport building. It involves practising, with conscious awareness, emotional regulation methods. It involves building in dialogue seminars as part of the operational calendar that the business operates within. Finally, it involves a career based on continuous personal growth and development with conscious awareness regarding one's inter- and intrapersonal skills to ensure our potential as leaders is fully developed.

Yes, leadership is not easy. However, the conscious leadership skills and methods reviewed throughout this book can be easily modelled and can substantially improve leadership/membership relationships. They just need to be practised so that they seep into our habits of mind, emotion and behavioural expressions and operate instinctively as our preferred modus operandi in terms of interactive leadership style.

The great transformational leader Mahatma Gandhi stated that: "*We but mirror the world. All the tendencies present in the outer world are to be found in the world of our body. If we could change ourselves, the tendencies in the world would also change. As a man changes his own nature, so does the attitude of the world change towards him*". Mahatma Gandhi was implicitly referring to role modelling and the broader principles of the butterfly effect as a metaphor for social and cultural change. This book and its ideas and methods resonate with this philosophy.

INDEX

Page numbers in italics indicate a figure and page numbers in bold indicate a table on the corresponding page.

Printed in the United States
by Baker & Taylor Publisher Services